The GOD WHO SMILES

SHERWOOD WIRT

D1052062

HARVEST HOUSE PUBLISHERS
Eugene, Oregon 97402

Cover by Koechel Peterson & Associates, Minneapolis, Minnesota

Also by Sherwood Wirt:
Jesus, Man of Joy

THE GOD WHO SMILES
Copyright © 2001 by Sherwood Eliot Wirt
Published by Harvest House Publishers
Eugene, Oregon 97402

Library of Congress Cataloging-in-Publication Data
Wirt, Sherwood Eliot.
    The God who smiles / Sherwood Wirt.
      p. cm.
    Includes bibliographical references and index.
    ISBN 0-7369-0436-0
    1. Joy—Religious aspects—Christianity. 2. God—Attributes. I. Title.

    BV4647.J68 W575 2001
    242—dc21   00-059758

Printed in the United States of America.

00 01 02 03 04 / RDP-MS / 10 9 8 7 6 5 4 3 2 1

CONTENTS

To my Grandnephew

Evan Sun Wirt

When our computer with its tricks
Consigned this volume to the Styx
Evan scanned, and all's restored
Praise the Lord!

Acknowledgment

"Of making many books there is no end," wrote the preacher, but this one may mark the end of what has been for me an exciting voyage on the literary Sea of Galilee. My shipmates—writers, editors, publishers, teachers—have proved to be not only able-bodied seaworthies and marine engineers, but have become cordial buddies and friends to steer me into port. For their help with this volume I would like to thank certain ones of those shipmates who are members of the San Diego County Christians Writers' Guild, and especially Nancy Bayless and Candace Walters.

This companion volume to *Jesus, Man of Joy* carries the discussion of a cheerful Christianity into the infinities of heaven and the mundane realities of life on planet earth. It is designed to introduce the smiling Lord God Almighty to contemporary mortals who might like very much to smile, and who may even believe in a God who smiles, but who amid the problems of the third millennium seem to be having trouble shifting their own joystick out of neutral.

I take this opportunity to express appreciation to my readers who have responded kindly to my 27 previous books, most recently to *Jesus, Man of Joy*. To the good people at Harvest House Publishers, I can certainly say that you have made book-publishing an experience of genuine joy. Finally, I may add that this present book would have never made it into print without the daily and hourly encouragement of my loving wife, Ruth Evelyn Love Wirt, *critiqueuse par excellence*.

A Creed of Joy

❧

God is the almighty, living, ruling Lord of all. He is one God, Father, Son, and Holy Spirit, who dwells in heaven, a place of eternal joy. As the psalmist says, "In thy presence is fullness of joy; at thy right hand there are pleasures for evermore."

God created the universe for His own pleasure and enjoyed doing it. He brought into being planet earth as an amazingly beautiful dwelling place for living creatures. He fashioned man and woman in His image to glorify and serve Him, and to live and rule in peace and joy in a garden. When He saw everything He had made, the totality of His creation, He smiled and called it "very good."

Something went wrong. Iniquity appeared, sin entered humanity with its curse, and earth became a place of sorrow, a troubled segment of the universe. Because God loves His children, He sent His Son, Jesus, to us by a virgin daughter of Israel, with a mission to free the earth from its curse and to return all its people from their burden of sin to an abundant life of love, joy, and praise.

To those who receive Him as Lord and acknowledge Him as Savior, Jesus Christ promised forgiveness, redemption from sin, a new birth, answers to prayer, the outpouring of His Holy Spirit of love, victory over death, and the everlasting joy of heaven. On a cross outside Jerusalem He kept that promise. "For the joy that was set before Him," Jesus bore our sins, accomplished our salvation, suffered and died and rose again to everlasting life in the kingdom of heaven.

Jesus lives today at the Father's right hand in resurrected glory and fullness of joy; and He has promised to come back for His church and to bring us where He is.

❧

THE UNIVERSE DELIGHTS IN GOD

1
DOES HE OR DOESN'T HE?

᠍᠍᠍᠍᠍᠍᠍᠍᠍

God is His own interpreter,
And He will make it plain.

—WILLIAM COWPER (1721–1800)

*B*efore attempting to write this book, I decided to ask myself some straight questions and try to answer them, questions such as:

"Do you think God smiles?"

"Yes."

"Have you ever seen Him smile?"

"No."

"How do you know He smiles?"

"I just know. And I smile back."

"How can you be sure it's God doing the smiling?"

"Because He is my Father. I feel His warmth. It's unmistakable, like the rays of the sun."

"Does the Bible say He smiles?"

"It says His face shines. A highly regarded translator renders Psalm 67:1, 'May thy face smile on us,' and Psalm 36:9, 'In thy smile we have the light of life.'"[1]

"Aren't you trying to glorify human behavior by putting human smiles into the heavens? Making up one of Freud's anthropomorphisms?"

"Who, me? Just the opposite. God created me in His image and likeness. He smiles, and so He made me able to smile."

"Why should He smile on you?"

"Ask Jesus. All I did was confess my sins and turn my life over to Him. He sent the Holy Spirit and the Spirit poured the love of God into my heart. Like that! Saved by grace through faith plus nothing! So He smiled and I smiled, and that was it."

"Aren't you a preacher's son?"

"I am. As a little boy I loved Jesus. Then I turned away from Him and became the black sheep in a religious family of six children. I stepped out of God's sunshine into the shadows."

"You mean He stopped smiling?"

"Just toward me. When I finally caved in at age 31, I felt His smile again. But my life as a believer took some hard turns, and I became disappointed, bogged down in self-pity and despair, until I even wished I was dead. But God brought me again to a place I once knew called Golgotha, and He broke my spirit there and filled me afresh with His own Spirit of love. Then the smiles came back."

"Whose smiles?"

"His and mine."

So welcome to *The God Who Smiles,* not only the last of my books, but also the first in the new millennium. If I catch aright the direction of the Holy Spirit's movement in His authentic and genuine churches today, I might say prophetically that you are heading toward something great. A new friendship in Jesus is evident among Bible-committed church leaders. No doubt the new century augurs its share of perilous dilemmas and frightening possibilities for humanity. But I believe it also carries the hidden promise of a fresh revival of the mercy, truth, and righteousness of Almighty God, and new hope among us all for His peace and brother- and sisterhood.

This third millennium, like the second, is under the dispensation of the Holy Spirit. It may reveal an aspect of the true God not always comprehended by past generations: His tender love and exquisite charm. That leads me to say to my younger fellow Christians as they begin their pilgrimage through the new century, "Ignore the present wave of cynicism. Be of good cheer. You are heading toward something great, something different, something as radiant as the sun." Or to render it in my favorite expression, "There is a God who smiles."

Not everyone agrees with me. Why should they? I was interviewed on a Christian television station in Chicago and was handed questions like these:

"You speak of God having a smile on His face. We don't often think of God that way, do we?"

"Do Christians really understand what the Joy of the Lord is all about?"

"Many people in North America feel as though there is nothing to be joyful about. What would you say to these people?"

You can see why I had to write this book. What a bowl of uncracked nuts! Replying to such queries has required thought, time, research, and even that quaint ancient custom that we Christians call prayer. That is why I tried to sketch out a "creed" at the beginning, so it will be clear that my theology is as straight as my mother-in-law's Bible could make it, she being my mentor. I should add that my spiritual life has been strengthened by learning the creeds of the church and has even been embellished by a thought or two that could have dropped down from the Original Source.

"But seriously, why the title?"

Well! First, God's presence is everywhere, but His dwelling place is heaven, which is also the dwelling place of everlasting gladness and joy. Right at this moment I believe He is smiling down on us human beings who populate the planet earth. There is a verse in John 3 that begins with the words, "God so loved the world." Why does He "so love"? Because that is the kind of God we have. He certainly does love the world and He loves us.

Then second, I believe He is the God who smiles because all joy comes from Him. He is the Source. Who else? No other place or source has ever existed from which true, genuine joy could come. I call it unfortunate that most theological textbooks written by Christian scholars fail to include joy as an attribute of Almighty God. They say God is infinite, eternal, immutable, illimitable, immortal, all-wise, all-knowing, all-good, holy, sovereign, just, righteous, merciful, and true. But *not* joyful. The word joy is ignored, and that is wrong, for joy is a very special divine attribute. Where on earth did joy come from? It didn't. It came from heaven.

Third, the visit that Jesus Christ, God's Son, paid to planet earth 2000 years ago confirmed God's love for the entire human race. Jesus proclaimed the kingdom of God. He sought to bring us back from sin and despair to life abundant through His death and resurrection. He promised to fill us with His Holy Spirit of love and never to forsake us. And to it all He added the promise of His own joy.

While Jesus was here, He taught that He was the true vine and His followers were the branches. I'll have more to say about that. Then He explained His purpose in some magnificent words in John 15:11: "These things I have spoken to you, that my joy may remain in you, and that your joy may be full."

What a stunning expression! It clarifies the full meaning of the term "the Joy of the Lord." Joy began in heaven with the Father's smile, came to earth with the Son, and is preserved for us as a fruit of the Holy Spirit. To be sure, joy itself was not the cause or purpose of Christ's being with us, but its presence has shed a permanent glow upon the whole miracle of the Incarnation.

Now for the human side of the picture. We live in an atmosphere that is far from perfect. Sin has blurred the evidences of a loving God in our midst. As the reformers used to say, the earth is not an evil thing, but a good thing spoiled. Trapped in the dross of sinful corruption on earth is the human concept of divine joy itself. That accounts for much of the sad, disturbed state of human society at the beginning of third millennium.

Yet don't count God out, or God's children either. We have found that even in today's declining moral climate there are some enjoyments utterly worthwhile and accessible to believers. What W.S. Gilbert called "innocent merriment" in his day can still be found in the new millennium, as engaging as ever and still never going over the line. (Consider, if you will, a piece of banana cream pie. I mean, just look at it: something beautiful, something good. Not "heavenly" in a literal sense, perhaps, but certainly delicious. Taste it!)

So what is our goal in this book? A joyous slice of pie? Not exactly. Richard, bishop of Chichester (1197–1253), is still remembered for his benediction: "May we see Thee more clearly, love Thee more dearly, and follow Thee more nearly." To which I would add, "And now, for heaven's sake let us who believe in Him stand up, shout for joy, and take God's clear word of the joy of salvation to the rest of humanity. And let us do it quickly, before the end comes, or even before the Internet transmogrifies everything on the earth's crust into gambling, pharmaceuticals, and smut."

Like most of you, I find the Joy of the Lord a very elusive quality, but I love writing about it. If you wish to join me on this merry-go-round, I will do my best to provide entertainment. As you will learn, strange things sometimes happen even on merry-go-rounds.

2
WHAT IS THE GREAT JOY?

❧

Joy is the gigantic secret of the Christian.
—GILBERT CHESTERTON

In *Jesus, Man of Joy,* which appeared in 1999, I made the point that a special kind of joy was and is displayed in the gospel of Christ. From its beginning in the song of the angels at Jesus' birth, to the joyful farewell prayer meeting after Jesus' disciples left the Mount of Ascension, this joy keeps surfacing and is highly visible, as in Luke 2:10 and 24:52. Thus our calling as Christians is to proclaim the message of the Lord Jesus Christ as *good news*—great news—great joy—and to evangelize, convert, disciple, and commission new believers. They are to nourish themselves on the living Word and then spread it.

But before we train these messengers and dispatch them into the new millennium, should we not first introduce them to the sparkling waters of joy that Jesus promised? To lead a person to the Savior and forget the Savior's joy is—well, it's odd. It's like scraping the frosting off the wedding cake and dropping the kiss from the marriage ceremony.

As a Christian journalist, I wholeheartedly support the faithful messengers who undertake the work of evangelism and tutelage and church-planting at home and abroad. Yet I see increasing evidence at many a church that somehow, in the ongoing hum of well-oiled ecclesiastical machinery, we have solemnly expounded the Christian message and then *dropped out* the joyous note of Jesus' gospel.

Alexander Schmemann of the Greek Orthodox Church writes, "From its very beginning Christianity has been the proclamation of joy. It announced and conveyed a new all-embracing joy, and without the proclamation of this joy Christianity is incomprehensible. It is only as joy that the church was victorious in the world, and it lost the world when it lost that joy. Let us forget for a while the technical discussions about the church, its mission, its methods. They can be useful and meaningful only within the context of the Great Joy from which everything else developed."[1] I don't know why, but as I read those splendid words, a saucy tune of my youth came to me: "It don't mean a thing if it ain't got that swing!"

The Bible message has a supernatural character so powerful and a timeless aspect so awesome that it keeps slipping beyond the limits of rational inquiry. As Isaiah reports to us, God's thoughts are not our thoughts. The Bible faithfully reflects the glorious, boundless scope and sweep of the Holy Spirit. The joyful message comes ringing down the corridors of time with words of mercy and love that telescope the centuries and fill us with a promising hope for the future. I confess that a feeling very close to ecstasy overtakes me personally when I lean back and reflect on the majesty and holiness of God, then pinch myself when I realize He is actually smiling on me.

Let's listen to God as He speaks in the book of Job and sends thundering words toward Job himself: "Where were you when I laid the foundations of the earth?…Surely you know!"[2]

What a question! But the Father may have modulated His tone when He next asks (I believe He was smiling), "Where were you when the morning stars sang together, and all the sons of God shouted for joy?"[3] In each case there is no response from Job—but one catches something highly amusing about the scene. God was apparently enjoying

Himself. And I'm just glad it was Job who was on the spot. Had it been yours truly—well, I would have just died!

While Sir Fred Hoyle and his fellow scientists continue to dispute over a "big bang" as the origin of creation, our passage in the book of Job seems to point rather to a great celebration. Cynthia Wilson-Felder, worship leader in an Atlanta church, is quite certain that is what happened. She says of the songs of the morning stars, "It was a party." Of the Genesis account she exclaims, "In the creation story, God was having a ball, telling things to 'be.' After He created each thing, God said, 'That's good.' When humanity came forth, His Word was, 'It's all good.' God was just having a wonderful time. It was real joy for Him."[4]

By contrast, I have been dipping into the life of Friedrich Nietzsche, the famed German philosopher, who died in 1900. It seems his writings provided the theme and set the stage for Adolf Hitler and the ghastly horrors of the Nazi revolution. Nietzsche grew up in a pious, cheerful German family and was well-educated. When he left home, he also left behind almost the entire philosophical and ethical structure of European civilization, including value concepts such as love, truth, goodness, and beauty. He became an atheist and boldly pronounced the demise of God. After ridiculing other motives for human behavior such as altruism and the drives for success and wealth, he maintained he had found the strongest and most effective motive of all, namely, the *will to power*. This conclusion led Nietzsche to develop his concepts of the "superman," the "blond beast," and the "master race" of white "Aryans." Conversely, he despised what he called the "slave society" of Christians, nonwhites, and especially Jews.[5]

This sick and infamous philosophy was later crucial in forming Adolf Hitler's thinking. Thus it helped to create the Nazi monster and led eventually to the murder of six million Jews. (I received a vivid impression of the fruit borne by Nietzsche's cruel doctrine of "forcible self-assertion" when I attended the 1961 holocaust trial of Adolf Eichmann in Jerusalem.)

Nietzsche's Achilles' heel was his total ignorance of a motive even stronger than will to power that exists in the cosmos, a motive that was created and established by God Himself. That motive was and is God's own divine love. His love established joy and peace in heaven and (when given a chance) is active today in human society, especially among His people. We "ordinary folk" draw from the Old and New Testaments the priceless love and the joy that the Bible contains—and we draw them particularly from the gospel message of Jesus Christ, where this love is written in His own blood. The same divine love can also be traced—if one knows where to look—in creation, in the stars and planets, in the colors of spring and fall, and in the natural movements of our beloved earth. It can be found in history in the holy lives of certain individuals. It is even embodied in the message of the last days, the *eschaton*.

All this is the gospel of God's love, the greatest force in the cosmos, and the most precious treasure of the human race. And this is what the Holy Spirit brings to us: joy unspeakable and full of glory.

Today Nietzsche, who once declared, "God is dead," is himself dead, a pitiful victim of venereal disease and mental breakdown. Unfortunately the naked will to power he worshiped is as strong as ever in our midst. New power struggles have broken out among military forces, scientific forces, economic forces, technological and environmental forces, religious forces, and (as the biblical writers prophesied and popular writers now declare) supernatural forces.

How does God's love stand a chance in the third millennium? No problem! There He is, seated serenely on His august throne, watching, knowing all things, and continuing to smile. He knows that today's greedy and selfish power brokers will try to take us the way of ancient civilizations, and like the Neros and Caligulas, they will in turn topple over each other and collapse.

When a new generation turns away from the divine commandments, disobeys its Lord, throws off restraint, and wreaks vengeance and cruelty on itself, then the smile of God does indeed disappear and judgment takes over. The prophet Ezekiel quotes the Lord God as asking, "When a righteous man turns away from his righteousness and commits iniquity, and does according to all the abominations that the wicked man does, shall he live?"[6] The New Testament letter to the Hebrews adds, "It is a fearful thing to fall into the hands of the living God."[7]

Yet God's wrath has never been the primary message of Christianity. His wrath is always reaction, never original action. On the heavenly scale, mercy towers above judgment. Thanks to our Lord Jesus and His gospel, we can accept by faith the greatest news in the universe: There is a God who smiles.

3

THE GLORIOUS CREATION

෨

*Love all God's creation, the whole and
every grain of sand in it. Love every leaf,
every ray of God's light. Love the animals,
love the plants, love everything.*

—FYODOR DOSTOYEVSKY (1821–1881)[1]

What a dazzling panorama is God's universe! What a glorious, magnificent sight when we look up at night, scanning the millions of visible stars that make up the Milky Way and the whole cosmos. There is the warrior Orion stalking his path across the sky. There we see the Pleiades or Seven Virgins mentioned in Job and the Great Bear, Pegasus, Perseus, the Chair of Cassiopeia, the magnificent Big Dipper pointing to celestial north....It makes one quiver. We are so overwhelmed we want to do something—sing a hymn, write a poem, weep for joy, praise the Lord, kneel, laugh, shout...

Wait a minute. I wish to withdraw. Who can do justice to the infinite grandeur and glory of God's creation? Someone else, not I, for I am not qualified to attempt the cosmic bit. Two semesters of astronomy at a state university do not qualify anyone to search the mysterious framework of the universe as it is seen today through the Hubble telescope. But I can say this, based on Scripture: I do believe that God created the universe for His own pleasure;[2] that He did it out of sheer joy, and that He is still smiling today as He surveys the height and depth and length and breadth of *all that is*. But that is a long way from understanding God's creation in terms of energy and mass and light-years.

Let's start again more modestly, restricting ourselves to the solar system in which we live and move. We may be parked on one of the smaller and less spectacular planets rotating around the sun, but we have something going for us none of the others can match. Almighty God chose this little globule called planet earth to be the theater for bringing into existence the *miracle of life*. What a magnificent achievement of creation that was! What joy it must have brought to the Creator! We who fly above the earth in a faster-than-sound airplane, looking down on the terrain and water below, can hardly begin to take in the artistry of God. What a Master of science, what a Voice for goodness, what a Fount of wisdom, and what a brilliant Poet! Who of us humans can sound the depth of tender care that went into the creation of this whirling ball we call home?

Whoa. Again, I must confess incompetence. I cannot look at the solar system with true cosmological understanding. Many who have spent their lives studying the planetary system have reached no spiritual conclusions whatever regarding its origin. Some have suggested that a kind of accidental near-collision of the sun with another star may have taken place. As a result, pieces of the sun were broken off, and they in turn went scattering giant chunks of hard celestial projectiles spinning through space, one smaller chunk being our own earth.[3]

All of this creative activity took place, it is presumed, without any God in sight, smiling or unsmiling; and without any suggestion of love, joy, or satisfaction on the part of anybody or anything. After wading through pages of such opinionating, I feel compelled to ask a question: How do we who have survived as far as Millennium III fit into such a scenario? How can the sun's rays, as they fall on the new blossoms of our spring tulips, reflect such beauty in our own back yard? How does the mockingbird warbling on our treetop fit his tune to the roar of solar projectiles in outer space? My lawn continues to grow and needs cutting; how does that happen on a barren chunk?

One question leads to another. Why is nature so beautifully consistent, if it wasn't the Creator's idea? Why do the seasons operate so punctually? (Of course one reason is that twice a year our planet's orbit on the ecliptic crosses the celestial equator; but why does it do that?) Why does our planet have a shield of heat that protects it from "projectiles"? Why are the earth's gravitational pull and temperatures just right for life here to exist? Why is our distance from the sun so accurately calculated for human survival? Why is the human brain superior to the finest computer? Why do birds and butterflies fly south in winter? Who told them to?

There is only one answer, and that answer is God.

He wrapped atmospheric bonds around our globe to shield us from harm. He filled the orchards with fruit and the fields with grain and the oceans with fish. He covered the mountains with trees and hid precious metals inside them. He dropped pure, life-giving water into the lakes and streams. He sent the sunshine and the rain, the snows and the green grass, that we might enjoy to the fullest during our brief sojourn on the planet earth. He designed pain to warn us not to hurt ourselves. He made clothing for our first parents. He ordained marriage to give us a golden fence and bunker against the quagmire of promiscuity and the wild beasts of deadly disease. And as He worked He smiled, for it gave Him pleasure.

Unless we understand the true, original purpose of God in creation, we will never fully feel, much less understand, the joy of His salvation. God did not create the human race in order to become its judge; rather He created it to become its Father. He wanted us to be His own family, for His personal interest and delight.

God did not invent murder, He invented friendship. He did not invent cruelty, He invented kindness. In other words, God's original script designed us specifically to love Him and one another, and to function on joy—His joy.

Perhaps if we turn back to God's Word, the Bible, we will gain a clearer understanding of what God's purpose was and is in creation. Here are some relevant quotations from the book of the prophet Isaiah, from the book of Psalms, and from the book of Revelation:

Thus says God the LORD,
Who created the heavens and stretched them out,
Who spread forth the earth and that which comes from it,
Who gives breath to the people on it,
And spirit to those who walk on it:
"I, the LORD, have called You in righteousness,
And will hold Your hand;
I will keep You and give You as a covenant to the people,
As a light to the Gentiles,
To open blind eyes,
To bring out prisoners from the prison,
Those who sit in darkness from the prison house."

—ISAIAH 42:5-7

O LORD, our Lord,
How excellent is Your name in all the earth,
Who set Your glory above the heavens!...

When I consider Your heavens, the work of Your fingers,
The moon and the stars, which You have ordained,
What is man that You are mindful of him?...
You have crowned him with glory and honor.

The heavens declare the glory of God;
And the firmament shows His handiwork.

—PSALM 8:1,3-5;19:1

The four and twenty elders fall down before him
    that sat on the throne,
And worship him that liveth for ever and ever,
And cast their crowns before the throne, saying,
Thou art worthy, O Lord, to receive
    glory and honour and power:
For thou hast created all things,
And for thy pleasure they are and were created.

—Revelation 4:10,11 (kjv)

"For thy pleasure!" Let me ask, How could the Almighty take genuine pleasure in all this creating, and never crack a smile? The elders in Revelation were right: God enjoyed making the cosmos, else He would not have made it. It was God's smile, in fact, that brought a new dimension of joy into the universe.

When we look at a beautiful skyline or some other artistic natural landscape, we have trouble reducing such a wonder to protons and electrons crashing into each other. The truth remains that natural beauty is from the hand of God Himself.

THE MESSAGE OF THE UNIVERSE

One of the encouraging signs of this new millennium is the fresh interest of the scientific community in evidences of "intelligent design" in the cosmos. Recent studies by Dr. Hugh Ross and others reflect a dissatisfaction with the "mechanistic" approach to the universe. More and more references are made to "indefinable factors" and "mysterious, unknown quantities." It seems there is "more out there" than the telescopes reveal; the universe is somehow "bigger" than originally thought. Einstein's discoveries about the nature of "bent" space have caused reappraisals of Newtonian theories and have made some scientists search afresh for traces of a possible supernatural presence in the "given."

Sir James Jeans, the noted British physicist and astronomer, wrote, "We discover that the universe shows evidence of a designing or controlling power that has something in common with our own individual minds. From the intrinsic evidence of his creation, the 'Great Architect of the Universe' now begins to appear as a pure mathematician. The stream of knowledge is heading toward a non-mechanical reality; the universe begins to look more like a great thought than like a machine."[4] That is a long way from the first chapter of Genesis, but it opens a door.

Let me tell you a strange story. In the summer of 1943, when the fate of the whole world was at stake in World War II, I was on the East Coast, trying desperately to get into the uniform of a chaplain in the United States Army. To qualify I needed one year of experience as a full-time pastor.

While awaiting a call to a church, I enrolled briefly as a summer graduate student at Princeton Theological Seminary. Having come from California, I reveled in the impressive traditional atmosphere. Right then the campus was crowded with distinguished visitors to a special week-long "school of theology" that was led by outside speakers. Dr. John A. Mackay, president of the seminary, was to give the closing address on Sunday evening.

On that last night I sat with other students in the balcony of Miller Chapel and heard from Dr. Mackay a statesmanlike presentation of the Christian gospel.

While I sat listening, a fellow student nudged me and pointed with his finger. Down in the midst of that dignified congregation was sitting none other than the world's greatest living scientist, Professor Albert Einstein, bushy hair and all. This was the gentleman whom *Time* magazine in 1999 proclaimed "Man of the Century." As we now know, the professor was living in Princeton that year while working on the first A-bomb. Why was he in church? You tell me.

Before entering the ministry I had been a newspaperman, and my journalistic instinct was aroused. This was too good to miss! At the close of the service I slipped downstairs and approached the small group gathered in the pews around the professor. I waited, and eventually he turned to me, and we shook hands. Remember, he was a Jewish scientist in an evangelical chapel. After introducing myself, not knowing what else to say, I asked him hesitantly, "Sir, what did you think of the address tonight?"

Professor Einstein looked at me, smiled, and answered softly, "Excellent. It was my own opinion in another language."

I never forgot those words. Einstein's reply calls to my mind a line from William Cullen Bryant's masterpiece, "Thanatopsis," which I once memorized in school. Bryant begins his poem with the words,

> To him who in the love of Nature holds
> Communion with her visible forms, she speaks
> A various language.

As we move into the new millennium, I feel like asking whether the universe isn't speaking "another language" of its own, apart from its molecular activity. Perhaps it really is larger than it looks (which is hard to imagine, since it is infinite), or perhaps it has some characteristics that have not yet been discovered. In any case, we do not need to join with Nietzsche or Bertrand Russell or J.B. Watson or B.F. Skinner or any of those who have tried to detach God from His universe.

As a distinguished Scottish psychologist, James Drever Sr., has written, "That time is past. Science now speaks in a different tone, acknowledging that scientific law...which treats the universe as a vast mechanism...is after all partial, abstract and unreal."[5] The Creator is alive and well, and He tells us so with every rising of the sun and every drop of rain that falls.

I believe that the message of the universe is a message of love from a God who is smiling and wants us to enjoy—really enjoy—His creation. That message might be communicated, not only in the sounds of nebular machinery, polar axles, and the stars' burning fuel, but in the spring breeze in our treetops and in the sacred melodies of our churches. There's music in the air! Light-hearted cadences of gladness. And to bring them to you in the incandescent, overwhelming joy of the Lord is the purpose of this book, so that what Jesus called "My joy" may become yours.

As for the creation itself, Pythagoras may have been right in saying that as the planets move in their orbits, they give voice to "music of the spheres" in a harmonious symphony. That sounds like the God who smiles! If there really is another language out there, one that Professor Einstein might have been alluding to, it must be spoken in heaven. That would be the Holy Spirit's language of love, and it would help to explain a lot.

4
GOD SMILES ON HIS WORD

This great book...is the best gift
God has given to man...But for it,
we could not know right from wrong.

—ABRAHAM LINCOLN

This present book is not a proper Bible study. It has one aim: to establish that there is a God in heaven who created joy, and that He is a God who smiles. Were it another scholarly chapter-and-verse treatise, I don't think it would tear you away from your favorite ball team's losing streak on television. What doth it profit an author to prove his point and lose his reader?

So let's settle the matter early. I will offer you two good examples of God's smiling in the New Testament. You can then have fun checking out all 27 books for the other examples, if you so desire.

First, we'll look at the words that God spoke from heaven during John's baptism of Jesus, an occasion that is recorded in Matthew, Mark, and Luke. Jesus underwent baptism, after which He prayed and "the heaven was opened. And the Holy Spirit descended in bodily form like a dove upon Him, and a voice came from heaven which said, 'You are My beloved Son; in You I am well pleased.'"[1]

Those four words "I am well pleased" translate the Greek word *eudokesa*, and my *Englishman's Greek New Testament* renders it, "I have found delight." Allow me to ask you, when one finds delight, what does one do? Smile? Usually; and since the Bible says we are all made in the image and likeness of the heavenly Father, I dare to suggest that God was Himself at that point smiling.

Second, I invite you to listen to the words God spoke at the transfiguration of His Son Jesus on the mountain, an event which also was recorded in all three Synoptic Gospels. Mark 9:7 reads, "A voice came out of the cloud, saying, 'This is My beloved Son. Hear Him!' " Those last two words are obviously imperative, for God seems to be speaking a command; yet there is nothing stern about what He said. It was all love, joy, and enthusiasm. God was eager for the people to listen to the good news His Son was there to proclaim. It was a very exciting moment. "Hear Him!" The statement actually was more appeal than command, and the appeal required a smile to go with it, did it not? "Hear Him and be born again!"

Well, not everyone will agree with me. Some scholars will dismiss me as another religious "enthusiast." That puts me in the same boat with our Lord Himself, of course, so I am right at home. Getting here took a long time, but today the unbelievable joy makes it all worthwhile.

For a contrast, let's look briefly to the unsmiling religious scene of my younger days. What would you think of a Bible teacher who spoke to his students as follows? "I want you to look at the Bible as no more inspired than any other ancient document. Treat the Scriptures not as holy, but simply as a random collation of Mideastern religious scrolls and scraps of papyri like any other."

In other words, study the Old and New Testaments pretty much as you would the scratchings on a broken potsherd.

The teacher was my professor back in the 1940s. He went on to discuss "false information, errors of fact, phony miracles, mistakes in copying, inaccurate genealogies, outdated rules of conduct and morality, biased accounts of military struggles, mistaken prophecies regarding Jesus, obtuse theological dissertations, incorrect poetry, crude prayers, sermons that were never preached, and slanted accounts of religious persecution." And there, he said in effect, is your Bible!

I am reminded of a word from Josh Billings: "The trouble with people is not that they don't know, but that they know so much that ain't so." My first reaction as a theological student was not to challenge the instructor's statements. Rather I took the usual route from *ad hoc* to *ad hominem* and asked, as the Athenians on Mars Hill once asked after hearing the apostle Paul, "Who in the world is this seed-picker?"[2] I thought further, *What school trained him? What does Jesus mean to him? And what church is paying his salary so that he can unload such teaching on us trusting, truth-seeking students?* One of my colleagues framed his own reaction one day in chapel with a dry riposte that created a stir. He said from the pulpit, "The road to hell is paved with the skulls of scholars."

Looking back on those years, the best judgment I can make is this: In that classroom at that moment God did *not* smile. As time has passed, I have learned to separate wheat from chaff and to look at the 66 books of Holy Scripture from a totally different perspective. I regard the Bible as unique in the history of literature. God Himself gave the Bible to the human race. Unlike other sacred documents, it is a superhuman, supernatural, super-cosmic gift of the Holy Spirit, who inspired the original men (and possibly women) writers and enabled them to write not only for their day, but for all time, including ours—we who are now entering the third millennium. With respect to the existence of other so-called holy books, there is no other document in the world quite like it.

As I reflect on the way missionaries in the past and church-planters in the present have brought the Word of God to the whole human race, I can see why God is still smiling. "Truth is in order to goodness," John A. Mackay used to say, and good people have braved the challenge of discreditors, confuters, and imitators for 2000 years. Especially since Johann Gutenberg put the first Bible into print, missionaries have been helped by tentmakers, explorers, circuit riders, camel drivers, doctors, nurses, teachers, evangelists, and plain men, women, and children who have carried the Bible to every corner of the planet.

Those messengers have brought salvation to kings, queens, and presidents, convicts and jailbirds, rich and poor, and every race and tribe. Today Bible bookstores are open in nearly every country of the world, and people of every religious background are visiting them and learning about the gift of salvation and the God who smiles.

My professor has long since gone to his reward, but his views are still in circulation. Here is how I would now try to answer him:

1. Those biblical accounts of Hebrew monarchs are both valuable and remarkably accurate. They provide important background for the study of early Judeo-Christian history.

2. The military victories and defeats recorded in the Old Testament not only teach valid history, they are evaluated according to eternal principles. Must men fight? The Bible does not lie or color the facts: It makes a clear moral judgment, and the world is better for it.

3. The poetry of the Bible ranks among the finest ever composed.

4. The prophecies of the Bible, many of which have been fulfilled, have become our spiritual maps of the future. They tell us how God looks at what's ahead, and provide information much more valuable than does, say, the second law of thermodynamics.

5. The prayers found in the Bible are of such devotional and spiritual depth that we continue to make them our own prayers today. They teach us how to concentrate, and more important, how to communicate with the one true God.

6. The preaching in the New Testament is magnificent. It is a model for those who proclaim the gospel message in the twenty-first century.

7. The theological discourses in the New Testament, as in John, Romans, Galatians, and Ephesians, are unsurpassable in the clarity of their presentations of the will and pleasure of Almighty God. To take one example, Romans 5:5 declares: "The love of God has been poured out in our hearts by the Holy Spirit who was given to us." Such thoughts are hard to improve upon in disclosing the depth of the riches of God's love in Christ Jesus.

8. The accounts of "religious persecution" are actually the keys to our salvation. They reveal the moral character of God as they describe the atoning death of our Savior. In the sufferings of Jesus we learn of the forgiveness of sin and the conquest of death, the resurrection and the empty tomb—in sum, again we behold the revelation of the love of God in Christ Jesus our Lord.

9. The miracles of the Bible do not need defenders like me. They have their own unique survival values, and highly intelligent people have acknowledged their divine origin through the centuries. Someone—it may have been John Donne—expressed it for me a long time ago: "God said it, Christ did it, I believe it, that settles it."

LOVE HAS CONQUERED

What then is the truth about the Bible? It is this: For those who believe it, the Bible is a love story with a joyful ending. Rather than a tome of wrath or judgment, it is a love letter directed to every human being today, telling the fascinating, intriguing, unimaginable story of God's love for the human race. What the Bible says about sin and evil and judgment and punishment is based not upon *God's* doings at all, but on God's reaction to *our* doings. When we violate His commandments, He sees and He responds.

In other words, the underlying message of the Bible is about God's love for *US*. For *US*, that is, the living! It is the shout of jubilation, the song of the Winner. It tells us that the battle of life has been won for us. The scoreboard tells the fact: We are on the winning side. Death has been defeated. The siege is lifted. The barricades on the road to glory have been removed. Life is an open gate. Love has conquered. Joy is ours. We're in! Hallelujah!!

How then do we receive into our hearts the Joy of the Lord, that delectable dessert after the hearty meat of the gospel? We let the holy Scriptures feed our souls, then we set out in the Spirit to gladden the heart of God by what we do, say, and think. We walk in God's ways and show His love by sharing it and spreading it to people everywhere, whatever their name or sign.

Yet there exists a well-known human behavior pattern with respect to joy that is perilous. It sports a longing for material things that wastes itself in wishful thinking, as people pile up their hopes on some tempting goal such as an SUV that seems to epitomize future joy for them. So often they fail; or when they finally do achieve their goal, the joy it promised seems to have slipped away from it, leaving behind a litter of empty expectations and disappointments. *C'est la vie!* How many tear-jerking novels have been ground out on that theme?

God's love is not like that. As we find it in the Bible, His love is communicated through something many people don't even like to think about: a cross. But the cross of Christ is durable stuff. It can take us unscathed through the valley of the shadow of death. It is equipped and presensitized to purge the presence of sin from a planet that has labored under its curse for thousands of years. Among the last words of the New Testament are these: "There shall be no more curse."[3]

Jesus brought a message of love and joy and peace into an environment overrun with danger from thieves and peril from invasion; where people were cheating and mistreating each other, fearful families were avoiding strangers, and Roman troops were dominating the landscape. Jesus said to them all, "Come to Me....My yoke is easy and My burden is light."[4] Even as He faced His own cross, He did it, we are told, for us.

GRASPING THAT WHICH LASTS

How then do we access the joy of the Lord? We don't. We set about dishing it out ourselves! Just as we parents love to hear expressions of gladness and appreciation from our children and grandchildren, so God the Father loves to hear our shouts and praises. He loves to hear about valor and bravery and courage and victory. He glories in it when we dare lift our hands and offer ourselves afresh to Him.

When we cease searching for His joy and start praying it up ourselves and giving it back to the Lord; when we yield up our lives, endeavors, loved ones, purses—everything—to Him, and start living for Him instead of old number one, then He will give each of us back a cup spilling over with the spiritual blessings of heaven. That is the secret that will start the splashing mountain stream of the Holy Spirit cascading toward us. Hallelujah!

When I was young, the carousels or "merry-go-rounds" in amusement parks were often built with a steel arm projecting toward the painted animals attached to the moving circular platform. This arm contained a large supply of brass rings that were dispensed one at a time to us children who came riding by. We would reach out to grasp them, then toss the brass rings one by one into a large container, and ride around and try again.

What we children knew, and what made it exciting, was that one of the rings was not brass but bright "gold"! If we were fortunate enough to snatch it, we held it tight and turned it into the operator, who then gave us a free ride.

Life is a merry-go-round in more ways than one, and we are all on it, riding our horses, tigers, and giraffes. On our circuits, God invites us to lean out and reach for the gold ring. We reach, but when we grab we find we have only come up with the brass. Brass, brass, brass, time after time. But if we don't keep reaching, we'll never get to the gold.

Brass sometimes shines like gold, but gold it is not. The secret is to keep reaching and to watch sharp among the brass for the gold and the free ride.

Now, an excellent children's sermon is in the making here, and it's all free with the price of this book! For in real life the gold ring is Jesus Christ, the everlasting Man, the key to heaven's joy, and the brass rings are the cheap, synthetic rivals that seem to shine like gold. Grab them, and they prove dull and worthless. Watch for the gold—it is a free ride for life and beyond, for it will take you clear to heaven. There's no disappointment. Jesus never fails!

As for me, young and footloose, I kept reaching and grasping for the brass. I remember at age 27 drifting down the Yukon River through Canada with a partner in a 16-foot rowboat, heading nowhere. One day we pulled our skiff ashore at an abandoned mission station. A few roofless wooden structures were still standing, and in one of them we found what had been a library. Picking out a few of the damp, soggy books, I began reading them as we drifted downriver toward Eagle, Alaska.

Among the books I found a Bible. I read it for half an hour and understood most of what it said, but it held no appeal. The italicizing of some words I found confusing, but as a whole the passage I read left me depressed. I found no easy yoke, no light burden, no gold ring, no joy, so I pitched the Bible into the river. It seemed to me I knew better how to live my life than that ancient volume did. Thus the book of life was sent to me from heaven, and I let it slip through my fingers. It was pure gold; I thought it was brass.

Do you think God up in heaven gnashed His teeth at what I did? You're wrong. He knew what was coming, and He smiled tenderly—and waited. That is the kind of God He is.

5

GOD SMILES ON HIS WARRIORS

*You therefore must endure hardship as a
good soldier of Jesus Christ.*

—2 TIMOTHY 2:3

*I*n the year 1966, I sat on the top row of an outdoor amphitheater at Camp Pendleton, California, as a guest of the military. Below me sat a large contingent of United States Marines, about to receive a final briefing before embarking for Vietnam. Our 18-year-old son was among them. As the commanding officer addressed his troops, I heard him say, "Men, I can't tell you where you are going, or what you will be doing, but I can tell you this: *You will be in a war.*"

As we have entered a new century and millennium, those words seem to be prophetic, especially for young Christians now facing life. Whatever kind of history is made, they will be in a war. More than a battle against rogue nations, drug kings, skinheads, or militiamen, Christian young men and women will find themselves engaged in a total war against the forces of sin and evil.

We know from Scripture that the unseen powers of darkness are continually seeking to destroy the human race. There is no letup or letdown, for Satan is continually on the attack. Every form, every aspect of goodness and righteousness in life ranging from little children to God Himself is under siege.

Anarchy and nihilism have taken to the streets with bombs and guns, and society itself is threatening to go berserk.

Just because this book centers on the God who smiles, it does not follow that it can ignore the spiritual battle now being waged for our planet. When translators gave us the words of the apostle Paul, "The weapons of our warfare are not carnal,"[1] they did not realize that the word "carnal" in that sense would disappear from the English vocabulary. "Carnal" comes from the same root as the word "carnivorous," or flesh-eating. What Paul meant was that we Christians do not fight spiritual battles with swords and spears, which are held in fleshy hands.

Ours is not a military engagement with ordinary firepower, it is a conflict with the forces of darkness and the unseen hosts of wickedness in heavenly places. It requires different matériel, different ordnance and armament. It does not mean our weapons are ineffective—exactly the opposite.

The Bible recognizes the devil's power. Jesus dealt with evil spirits, and the evil spirits themselves had no trouble recognizing Jesus as the Son of God. Today the evil forces, the "principalities and powers of darkness" are looking for new, popular ways to create hate and disaster, not only by launching racial and religious wars and poisonous plagues, but by subverting and corrupting the character of Christians and their families. No joy there!

Florence Nightingale, who came to Christ at 16 and became the magnificent pioneer of British military nursing, looked upon life as "a hard fight, a struggle, a wrestling with the Principle of Evil, hand to hand, foot to foot."[2] She added, "Every inch of the way must be disputed. The night is given us to take breath, to pray, to drink deep at the fountain of power." J.H. Oldham pointed out that "the writers of the New Testament see life as a warfare between the Kingdom of God and the powers of evil. Faith is a call to battle; it is the victory which overcomes the world. We prove our faith by sallying forth to meet the enemy."[3]

What are our weapons? They are the invisible armor of God, described in Paul's letter to the Ephesians: the belt of truth, the breastplate of righteousness, the shoes of the glad tidings of peace, the shield of faith, the helmet of salvation, the sword of the Spirit, and above all, prayer and supplication in the power of the Holy Spirit.[4] We are to put them on with eagerness and zest, as healthy men and women responding to combat.

JOY IN THE MIDST OF BATTLE

History tells us that men have always experienced a certain kind of excitement when going into battle. From time immemorial military leaders have recognized it, used it, and glamorized it in poetry and song. People still like to cheer their soldiers on parade, but today's victims of war's cruelties find little to cheer in military displays. The truth is that the coming of peace to a war-torn country is received with infinitely greater joy than a summons to war.

Unfortunately, we Christians find that the struggle against evil never ceases, and today the whole world has become a ship in a storm with a loose cannon on deck. If we are to find the joy of the Lord in this life, it will be in the midst of conflict and opposition, not in hiding. "In the world you will have tribulation;" said Jesus, "but be of good cheer, I have overcome the world."[5]

Here the war analogy cancels out. Jesus makes it clear that when we put on the armor of God, it is not a shell of protection to make us safe. A hermit's cave provides protection but no solution. Nor is God's armor used to attack or hurt other human beings. It is, in a word, simply equipment. It is a tool. When we ask someone to dig a hole, we provide a shovel.

When we put on the armor of God, the weaponry becomes a tool He has provided, an instrument for use on His job. What job? Taking the gospel of the living Christ to people and nations in the twenty-first century. What then are these weapons? Truth, faith, salvation, righteousness, prayer, and the Holy Spirit—and the joy of the Lord. Clothed in this armor, we become not invisible but invincible!

That's where the fun comes in. That's when we learn who is really running the show—the Holy Spirit Himself. That's when the home runs and touchdowns pile up. *Christus Victor* has taken over. We begin to see what the apostle Peter meant when he wrote of Christians exulting with "joy unspeakable."[6] We begin to understand the difference between enjoying the casual pleasantry of eating waffles after church on Sunday (which I happen to like) and reveling in the Joy of the Lord.

Dora Greenwell, a fine English Christian writer, expresses it this way: "Gradually, almost imperceptibly, the believer will find doors opening upon him, doors of happiness, doors of usefulness, which will be to him a gate of Heaven. Windows will open, letting in the breath of summer upon his soul, filling it with sunshine and sweet air. Suddenly some new interest, some friend will appear in the thick of battle. When Christ is lifted up within the believing soul, nothing is too hard for it to venture upon or endure. It rests upon a power beyond itself."[7]

Gilbert Chesterton said that when a man becomes a Christian he will do two things: He will dance, and he will fight. In the midst of that great moral struggle which every true Christian has to face, the Lord God Almighty has sent a beautiful token of His smiling presence. That is His joy. We find it in the most famous passage in the Bible, the 23rd Psalm. Here are the words (I use the King James reading): "Thou preparest a table before me in the presence of mine enemies: thou anointest my head with oil; my cup runneth over."[8]

There they are, the enemies, stationed all around us, mocking and threatening us, and what does the Lord do? He ignores them and proceeds to treat us like nobility. He can't seem to do enough for us. What a perfect expression of the delight our Lord takes in us, as He "prepares a table" for us and anoints us! And what a God!

As for the combat with evil itself, we find in Scripture a most unusual morale builder in the "Song of Deborah." It seems the Israelite soldiers called upon the prophetess Deborah to lead them against an invading Syrian army under General Sisera. She did, and after the battle Deborah composed and sang a jubilant song about the victory. In it she declared, "From the heavens the stars fought, from their courses they fought against Sisera."[9] Yes, the stars are on our side. That is the Joy of the Lord.

For a classic story of joy in battle, turn in the Bible to the book of Nehemiah and read the account of a famous Hebrew warrior and servant of the Lord who found himself in a war. The city of Jerusalem lay in ruins, its walls demolished and its Hebrew citizens crushed. At the time Nehemiah was far away in Shushan, a chief fortress of the Persian Empire, where he had risen in power to become cupbearer to the imperial ruler, King Artaxerxes.

One day Nehemiah's brother arrived in Shushan to pay him a visit and told him about the shocking conditions in Jerusalem. Nehemiah's reaction? He spent some time in prayer, then waited on his king with a request for a leave of absence. King Artaxerxes showed the effect of Nehemiah's influence on him by granting the request, appointing Nehemiah governor of Judea, and then giving him a military escort across the desert.

Upon arriving in Jerusalem, Nehemiah set about recruiting Hebrew men and women to repair the broken city wall. Resistance cropped up immediately from the Samaritan,

Ammonite, and Arab elements living in the city. Plots were drawn up to stop the work and kill the Hebrew workers. Nehemiah responded, according to the ancient record, by arming his crew of wall laborers "so that with one hand they worked at construction, and with the other hand held a weapon."

Nehemiah told the men, "Wherever [on the repair job] you hear the sound of the trumpet, rally to us there. Our God will fight for us." He added significantly, *"The joy of the LORD is your strength."*[10]

The joy element provided the strength and courage Nehemiah needed to finish the wall for the protection of Jerusalem. When we leap from the time of the broken wall of Jerusalem to the time of the broken wall of Berlin, we realize how history keeps repeating itself. The strength that comes from the Joy of the Lord proved effective in Nehemiah's day, and His power is still needed desperately in ours.

Look again at those words: "The joy of the Lord is your strength." What did Nehemiah mean by them? He seems to suggest that joy is more than piety, more than sincerity and earnestness. It is a secret power resource, something that Jesus had—an inexplicable, overwhelming gladness of heart. And will it come to us? Yes, as we become fully conscious of our heritage as children of the Most High. It comes as a shivering awareness of eternity, a healthy tingling in our blood, an unexpected elevation of spirit—a taste of the sacred elixir, as it were—best expressed, perhaps, by our own joyous laughter. Paul Rader used to say that "the anointing oil that Samuel poured upon the head of David put laughter into David's life."[11]

The Joy of the Lord is the excitement we feel—unmixed with the sorrow of earthly war—as we put on His armor, take the sword of His Holy Spirit, and step out on the field of the world to defy the enemy.

The Joy of the Lord becomes our strength as we sense a new flux of energy into our limbs to meet evil head-on and overcome the challenge of temptation.

The Joy of the Lord is ours when we lift His royal banner and declare to the whole human race our salvation from sin by the grace of God through the blood of Jesus Christ and His cross.

The Joy of the Lord brings our jubilation as we see the devil's aims and devices thwarted and frustrated, and his plans crushed into rubble, while he crawls back into his mouse hole.

The Joy of the Lord is our expression of triumph as we leave the battlefields of evil and go home to God with a shout of victory, and as we join God's people in marching before the throne of heaven.

The Joy of the Lord is our sense of victory in Christ as we set out by faith to win others to the greatest cause on earth, the cause of love that is the cause of our Lord Jesus Christ.

The Joy of the Lord is in our cheers every time we learn of a noble act of love or sacrifice or forgiveness, regardless of who did it.

The Joy of the Lord becomes our inexpressible reward when we, by the miracle of love, turn our enemies into friends and give the Holy Spirit access to new hearts and lives for the glory of God's kingdom.

This is the smile of God. This is Jesus, *Christus Victor,* who lifted the curse of sin from us, made our planet a place of great blessing, and rose from the grave to show us the way to life everlasting. As the late Professor Gustav Aulén of Sweden wrote, "The victory of Christ over the powers of evil is an eternal victory...The note of triumph rings out."[12]

6

God Smiles Through His Son

❧

These things I have spoken to you, that My joy may remain in you, and that your joy may be full.

—John 15:11

A friend walked past me and remarked in passing, "I'm having a terrible time with joy."

There was no appeal to me for help, which was a blessing, for I had no pious clichés to quote at the moment. But I couldn't help wondering afterward, *How many people in the world are having a "terrible time" with joy?* And the words of Jesus came to mind: "I will see you again and your hearts will rejoice, and no one will take your joy from you."[1]

That is a beautiful promise. It tantalized me, for I wanted very much to reassure my friend; but how to do it without invading privacy? The door was shut, and I now feel God will have to open it.

Later I went back over the passage in which Jesus faced the devil in the wilderness and was refreshed afterward by angels. I read how Jesus, filled anew with the power of the Holy Spirit, came into Galilee, declaring in what must have been an excellent, even a joyful mood: "The time has come....The kingdom of God is near. Repent and believe the good news!"[2]

But the verses did not seem to fit my friend's "terrible" mood. For a moment I wondered, *Is God really accessible when we need Him? What if He doesn't have a smile for some people?*

In a Christian bookstore a week later I saw the title, *The Attributes of God,* and bought the book—a reprint from several decades back, but in a new edition. It wasn't much help. It listed God's attributes, but joy was not among them. It also spoke of God as being "unknowable" in His "impassible solitariness." I recalled reading something like that years ago in Herbert Spencer's *First Principles.* He said if there is a God, He is "unknowable" both scientifically and religiously. (Spencer was a supporter of his fellow Englishman Darwin.)

Now I had to ask myself, *Is this true? Can't I know God? Don't I know Him?* I thought of Abraham and Moses. Did they not know God? And what about Job, and Elijah, and David, and Peter, and Paul? What about our Lord Jesus Christ?

It was back to the Scriptures again. There I found both Abraham and Moses were called friends of God. The Bible certified that God is the Father of our Lord Jesus Christ, that He loves us all, is not at all distant to us, and wants the fellowship of His children. What a relief! I found friendship, affection, and warmth.

The Bible, from one viewpoint, is the story of divine help to us. God performed a miracle that got the Israelites across the Red Sea in their flight to freedom. He helped Joshua find a home for the nation. He sent His Son Jesus to bring a message of the joy of salvation not just to Israel, but to the whole world. And ever since God has been helping, helping, helping tribes and races and nations and churches and bringing people peace and love and joy for generation after generation, right down to the end of the second millennium. We have a great cloud of witnesses to prove it. That's the kind of God He is: not unknowable but knowable, not joyless but full of joyance.

People who are having trouble connecting with the Joy of the Lord should try excavating the rich ore of the Bible. I found 542 references to joy in its pages, which would include gladness (141), delight (85), pleasure (70), laughter (40), merry (30), happy (27), and a host of references in the newer

Bible versions to exuberance, jubilation, merriment, rapture, elation, bliss, and other synonyms for joy. In the Psalms alone I found 105 expressions of joy. The four Gospels, the book of Acts, and the letters of Paul, Peter, and Jude proved equally fruitful. In other words, any thorough seeker will make the incredible discovery that the Bible is a book of joy, and is running over with it. My question was: Which of the 542 references to joy made it available to someone like my friend who was "having a terrible time" with it?

I have thought of the tremendous blessings that Jesus brought to the human race over two millennia of history. Captain Eddie Rickenbacker, whose record for downing German planes in World War I made him one of the twentieth century's heroes, told me, "If it had not been for Jesus Christ, there would never have been an America." That statement could be expanded to spread over many another nation. What would the world be like if there were no Sermon on the Mount? What if there were no Christmas story? No parables of the Good Samaritan and the Prodigal Son? No "love" chapter in First Corinthians? No Lord's Prayer? No hope in the empty tomb?

Faithful Christians have repeated these classic New Testament passages millions of times over the past two millennia. Invariably they bring a smile to an unhappy face, a lift to a depressed spirit, a word of praise to a beleaguered heart. They tell us what we cannot see but what we earnestly want to know: that there is a smile on the face of God in heaven. For that we can thank His Son. And yet somehow the masses of people are not responding. Our win-a-million generation seems to turn down the corners of its mouth; the final answer to the challenge of the new day is disappointment.

Charles Colson writes, "The opening decade of the millennium [should be] a cause for jubilation....yet my sense is that most Christians are anything but jubilant."[3] He is right, and it's very sad. God's word to Jeremiah still holds: "You will seek Me and find Me, when you search for Me with all your heart."[4]

But what if people don't know what to search for, or how or where to look?

What could I say to this friend who was having a terrible time with joy? Should I pray and perhaps weep? Should I try gaiety? What about earnestness? Or even golf? There is a kind of joy that comes with great athletic strain. There is a joy of achievement, and a joy that comes with deliverance from the bad and the ugly. There is a joy that comes with the unexpected and the exceptional, a joy when a new thought seizes the mind, a joy when the mind changes its attitude from negative to positive, a joy when the heart falls in love, and a joy when right triumphs over wrong. Would something like that work? (People tell me there can even be joy in suffering, but if it be true, I hope it stays earthbound.)

Most of these joys can be deemed pale reflections on earth of heaven's own joyance, and we can thank God for them, for they brighten up our lives most wondrously. However, we are after bigger game. We are in search of the Joy of the Lord, the joy that Jesus brought to earth. We are looking for rapture that comes from God Himself, as He smiles on His beloved. How to capture this bright jewel from heaven, this joy thing that is but isn't—how to revel in it, and to pass it on?

I felt very foolish and incompetent, until in my bafflement I remembered something Andrew Murray had written a long time ago, something about Jesus and a grapevine.

HIS LIFE, HIS JOY

Andrew Murray was a Scotsman who pastored a church in South Africa and became a writer of great spiritual power and worldwide influence. He was 88 years old when he died in 1917. All of his writings had to do with the Scriptures. My godly mother-in-law collected the paperback editions of his works, and some of them are still in my library.

In some excitement I found one titled *The True Vine* and turned immediately to the chapter titled "Joy." It discussed

John 15:11, which has Jesus saying, "These things I have spoken to you, that My joy may remain in you, and that your joy may be full." I had a feeling my search was over. A "terrible time with joy"? Listen to this.

The first thing Pastor Murray said was, "Our Lord's words are, 'You cannot have My joy without My life.'" (Why hadn't I thought of that?) He quoted further, "'Abide in Me, and let Me abide in you, and My joy will be in you.' All healthy life is a thing of joy and beauty." (What wisdom!) "Live undividedly the branch life, and you will have His joy in full measure." (I knew what he meant by the "branch life" because Billy Graham's mother, Mrs. Morrow Graham, had used the expression when I interviewed her for *Decision* magazine. It is a reference to Jesus' statement in the same passage, "I am the vine, you are the branches."[5] The branch life is a life filled with Jesus.)

"To many Christians," Murray went on, "the thought of a life wholly abiding in Christ is one of strain and painful effort. They cannot see that the strain and effort only come as long as we do not yield ourselves unreservedly to the life of Christ in us. Jesus is saying, 'I ask nothing of the branch but that it yields wholly to Me, and allows Me to do all.'"

I felt I was trespassing on holy ground. I read on:

"We are to have Christ's own joy in us. And what is Christ's own joy? There is no joy like love. There is no joy *but* love. His joy is nothing but the joy of love, of being loved and of loving. It was the joy of receiving His Father's love and abiding in it, and then the joy of passing on that love and pouring it out on sinners. It is this joy He wants us to share. His joy will be ours, the joy of loving like Him, of loving with His love.

"Christianity is meant to be in everyday life a thing of unspeakable joy. Why do so many complain that it is not so?" (This was written a full century ago!) "Because they do not believe that there is no joy like the joy of abiding in Christ and in His love. Let the truth enter deep into us. As long as our joy is not full, it is a sign that we do not know our heavenly Vine aright; *every desire for a fuller joy* must only urge us to abide more simply and more fully in His love.

"As the Vine, so the branch; His divine joy is our joy."[6]

Such was the message God gave me about His Son. Some words of Rees Howells on the same subject seemed to confirm its meaning:

"Self (as self) can never abide in the Savior...yet the Vine can't do anything without the branch. All the sap of the Tree is running through the branch. And when this new life flows through us, every bit of us tingles with it, even our very body itself. If the Vine has joy, the branch has the same joy, and the needy get the fruit."[7]

Now for a special word: I know you have probably heard it all before, but pause just for a moment. This is not tiddly-winks. You are standing on holy ground. Ask yourself, "Where is my joy?" Then take off your shoes (not necessarily physically) and stand with your bare feet on Calvary Road. Then move out to the cross of Jesus, taking with you your unhappy bag of peccadilloes. You will meet God there, the lovely God, the merciful God who saves and forgives and heals. He will greet you with a smile. Jesus will meet you there, radiating love and joy. He is the One who told you to be of good cheer. He is the One with marks on His hands. Once the debris of your life is blown away by the clean, strong wind of God's love, the Joy of the Lord will come; and Jesus' word to you is that *no one will take it from you.*

God is not mean, nor is He solitary. He is a God who loves you, and He will give you back your joy and keep you smiling. How do I know? Not just because it has happened to so many others, but because it happened to me.

7

God Smiles on His House

∾

I went with them to the house of God,
With the voice of joy and praise.

—Psalm 42:4

God enjoys worship. He takes pleasure in the adoration and praise of His children when it is free, untrammeled, voluntary, loving, and warm. He accepts it gladly because when we are worshiping Him in Spirit and in truth, we are not wasting His time or ours in adulating ourselves or each other.

He smiles when we worship Him in solitude, and He smiles when we gather together to sing, pray, and call upon His name. Whenever a body of worshipers puts other things aside and simply concentrates on speaking with God in terms of love, singing praises to Him, and earnestly seeking His face, you can be sure He is smiling. It makes no difference what the size of the group or where it is meeting.

This chapter will not discuss the varieties of worship in the church as a whole. During years of travel with Billy Graham I encountered many differences in the ways Christians make their approach to the King of heaven. It was a pleasure and an honor to join these brothers and sisters and participate in their worship. I have no way of knowing how God Himself feels about our traditional differences in prayers and liturgies. I respect them all, knowing that they draw many to Jesus.

For a few moments we might try looking at God's house as God might look at it. Not at the steeple. Not at the prayer books or the hymnals or songsheets or the various orders of worship, but rather at the people who are drawn to God and are gathered together in His house. What kind of communication is taking place between them and God? Are they feeling guilty, while conscientiously reflecting on their sins? Are they being reconciled to the God of peace, loving Him and telling Him so? Are they basking in the sunshine of His divine love, knowing that God Himself is smiling on them right where they are?

What is going on?

Abraham, the human father of the Hebrew race, did not build a house for God. He worshiped at an altar by the terebinth of Mamre, a spreading tree not unlike an oak. Moses, centuries later, received from God on Mount Sinai a pattern for a holy tabernacle. It became a portable structure that the Israelites carried on their travels until they arrived in Canaan. Centuries later David, king of Israel, expressed a desire to build a noble temple that would be honored as God's "house." It was actually erected by his son, Solomon. At its dedication King Solomon offered a prayer to God that included these words: "Behold, heaven and the heaven of heavens cannot contain You. How much less this temple which I have built!"[1] Some humor there!

In the centuries that followed, the Jerusalem temple was honored again and again in psalms and stories, many of which are included in the Old Testament. Poets and prophets have declared it the most sacred spot in the whole world, the beating heart of the faith of God's people, wherever they may live. Jesus Himself described it as a place of prayer. Yet Jesus created a sensation that resulted in His arrest when He spoke of His own body as a "temple" that would be "raised up" in three days.[2] Paul went further with the analogy by asking the Christians of Corinth, "Do you not know that your body is the temple of the

Holy Spirit who is in you, whom you have from God?"[3] What a doctrine to get people excited!

During the time of His ministry, Jesus' worshipers simply gathered wherever He was. After the resurrection and ascension, Jesus' followers began to meet on the Lord's Day for worship and prayer, sometimes in fields, sometimes in upper rooms, in private homes, or in schools or synagogues. As new converts, the early worshiping community of believers began to be known as "The Way," and their meeting place, wherever it might be, was still God's house. Jesus had told them simply, "Where two or three are gathered together in My Name, I am there in the midst of them."[4]

A form of worship soon began to develop around the holy meal called "the Lord's Supper," which they ate "with gladness," and the holy sacrament of baptism, symbolizing "the washing of regeneration" that comes with salvation. New joyous songs were composed and prayers took form as part of the young church's life. The Gospels were written and circulated from house to house and city to city and even from country to country. Yet the members of the gathering known as "The Way" still found that there was no substitute for personal worship (such as Jesus practiced). Individual worship, a blissful meeting alone with and talking with God "one on One" wherever the believer happened to be, was essential to the final, basic fabric of Christian faith, and for 2000 years it has yielded the richest of blessings.

Over 20 centuries, thousands of churches, including all the magnificent Gothic cathedrals, have been raised up to the glory of the Triune God. It has been my unexpected privilege to visit St. Isaac's Cathedral in St. Petersburg, Russia; Westminster Abbey and St. Paul's in London; Paris' Notre Dame Cathedral; the Cologne Cathedral in Germany; St. Andrew's in Sydney, Australia; and many other beautiful churches around the world.

Yet as I read the Bible, God, the Creator of life, though He is the Origin of beauty, seems far more interested in joyful people than in brick and mortar. To put it another way, a human being can become, according to the New Testament, a living temple to God; but an empty church, for all its holy atmosphere, can become a box.

God's house, your house, my house, or no house at all—from the eternal perspective, does it matter? When the communication between human beings and heaven is genuine and sincere and filled with joy, and worship is taking place as the Bible teaches us, we can be sure that God is present. As Peter wrote to the Christian believers of Bithynia, Cappadocia, and other parts of what is now Turkey, "You also, as living stones, are being built up a spiritual house, a holy priesthood."[5]

JOY COMES FROM ENCOUNTERING THE LIVING GOD

There are those Christians who have been blessed with unusual experiences of God's presence in worship—not always in a sanctuary—that seem to transcend time and space. I am not one, for my sins; but I have been fascinated to read what has happened to others. They have been taken into realms of the mind that the computers will never penetrate. Like Sidney Lanier, we all wonder at life's deeper mysteries and yearn to "build our home on the greatness of God."

The apostle Paul was one such visionary, and his strange visit to the third heaven, which he described in the twelfth chapter of his second letter to the Corinthians, is worth one's reading. Paul has given us mundane believers a glimpse into the mysteries of the Great Unknown that whets our appetites for more. He wrote as if the experience happened to another man, but it was obviously Paul himself who was "caught up into Paradise and heard inexpressible words."

Not so well-known is the experience of Henry Suso (or Seuse), a German of the duchy of Swabia, who entered the

Dominican order very young and at 18 years underwent a spiritual conversion. Soon afterward a "happening" occurred to him that his autobiography describes. Like the apostle Paul, Suso used the third person to describe it. Here are his own fascinating words:

> It happened to him while a "beginner," that he came into the choir on Saint Agnes' day after the midday meal of the community. He was there alone and stood in the lower stalls of the right choir. In these days, he was sorely afflicted with a burden of grief that weighed down upon him. As he stood there disconsolate, with no one to comfort or to help, his soul was caught up in rapture, whether in the body or without the body. And he saw and heard what no tongue can ever tell. It was without form, without mode, and yet it had within itself the gladsome blessedness of all forms and modes. His heart was panting, and yet satisfied; his spirits were joyful and blooming; longings were stilled in him, and desires extinguished.
>
> He gazed into the glowing radiance in which he lost his awareness of self and of all things. Was it day or night? He did not know. It was a gushing forth of the sweetness of eternal life felt as present, in a motionless, silent experience. He said afterward, "If this was not Heaven, I do not know what Heaven is." This ecstatic spell lasted maybe an hour, maybe half an hour. When he came back to himself, he felt like a man who has come from another world.
>
> He went his way. No one saw these things, or noticed anything about him. But the powers of his soul were filled with the sweet fragrance of Heaven. This heavenly fragrance remained with him a long time afterward, and gave him a heavenly desire and yearning after God.[6]

"Gladsome blessedness." Does that tell us something about the Holy Spirit, or doesn't it?

A spiritual experience not too different occurred late one evening to the French writer Blaise Pascal. He, as a scientist, wrote it down, and when he died at age 39 in 1662, his notes were found sewn into his coat. I have chosen just a few expressions from his description of an encounter with the living God:

> In the year of Grace, 1654, on Monday, 23rd of November...From about half past ten in the evening until about half past twelve. FIRE!
>
> God of Abraham, God of Isaac, God of Jacob, not of the philosophers and savants.
>
> Certitude. Certitude. Feeling. *Joy.* Peace...
>
> God of Jesus Christ. My God and your God.
>
> Your God shall be my God.
>
> Forgetfulness of the world and of everything, except God.
>
> He is to be found only by the ways taught in the Gospel.
>
> Greatness of the human soul.
>
> "Righteous Father, the world has not known You, but I have known You."
>
> *Joy, Joy, Joy, tears of joy.*
>
> I have fallen away from Him.
>
> I have departed from Him.
>
> "They have forsaken me, the Fountain of living water."
>
> My God, will You forsake me?
>
> May I not be separated from Him eternally.
>
> "This is life eternal, that they might know You, the only true God, and Jesus Christ, whom You have sent."
>
> Jesus Christ.
>
> Jesus Christ.

I have fallen away: I have fled from Him, denied Him, crucified Him.

May I never be separated from Him!

We keep hold of Him only by the ways taught in the Gospel.

Renunciation, total and sweet.[7]

Dante Alighieri, whose *Divine Comedy* is often described as the world's greatest poem, brings his wanderings in hell to a close and gives us a magnificent climax in his final cantica, *Il Paradiso.* As translated by Dorothy Sayers, Canto 27 contains the lines:

"To Father and to Son and Holy Ghost,"
All Heaven broke forth, "Be glory!" Such sweet din,
My sense was drunken to the uttermost;
And all I saw, meseemed to see therein
A smile of all creation; thus through eye
And ear I drew the inebriate rapture in.
O joy no tongue can tell! O ecstasy!
O perfect life fulfilled of love and peace![8]

Yes, it comes to people—a personal visitation from God! Nothing so glorious ever touched my life, yet there came a quiet day not long after an "Afterglow" prayer meeting when I knew something was forever different. I was smiling! I had nothing against anybody anywhere; my problems ceased to exist, my long bitter ode to life evaporated in God's sunshine. I had been to the cross, had known soul crucifixion, and now I loved everybody.

Talk to God? Yes. Response from God? Yes! Yes! Jesus is alive! "In Your presence is fullness of joy"![9] Embrace it. Bask in it.

The God who smiles offers us inner joy here on earth now and forever through Jesus Christ. I don't mean happiness. (Happiness has been defined as the look on a dieter's face on reaching the desired weight and heading for a restaurant.) Inner joy is something deeper. It comes "trailing clouds of glory."

Billy Sunday once declared, "If you have no joy, there's a leak in your Christianity somewhere." Jesus gives that joy. We don't have to wait for heaven to find it. And when we do find the inner joy that Jesus brought, let's not keep it to ourselves. Let's sing and shout it.

8
GOD SMILES IN THE STARS

≈

"Why can't we all just get along?"

his incongruous voice from the streets came to me
sometime during the late years of the twentieth century. I can
still hear it, for it reminded me of a different, equally incongruous voice I heard while drifting down the Yukon River in a
rowboat back in 1938. My two traveling partners and I had just
passed a cut blazed in the steep banks that marked the
boundary between the United States and Canada. Suddenly we
heard a piercing scream, agonizing and terrifying, coming
from the thick overgrowth far up on the hillside. It sounded
like a woman's voice, and was followed by a chorus of fierce
barking and yelping. Then once again came the primeval
silence. We guessed that we had heard a wolf pack surprising
a deer, and the pitiful cry was the deer's dying utterance.

What did the scream say to us about life on earth? About
pain and fear and life and suffering and fate? We drifted on
downriver, brooding about creatures like that pathetic deer,
each wondering in his own way, *Why can't we all just get
along?*

The prophet Amos uttered a word similar to the above
expression about "getting along" 2800 years earlier. He asked,
"Can two walk together, unless they are agreed?"[1] It sounds so
easy. Why is it then so difficult for us human beings to put our
egos out to pasture and achieve really good relationships?

That puzzler presupposes a deeper question that we find almost unanswerable, given the facts: Why does a good, loving, smiling God allow cruelty and evil on our planet? If, as we Christians insist, God is love, why has such a blight been allowed to afflict human and animal life? There's more to the question than asking, "Why can't we get along?" We must go on and ask questions such as, "Why did God permit the wolves to inflict such a cruel death on the deer? What's wrong with the *world?*"

If we think our lack of willpower has something to do with the problem, we flatter ourselves. Willpower can help us, but more is required. If we think the problem of evil is caused by "something in the air" or "something in the water," we are equally mistaken. Finding the answer to the problem of sin and evil is *the greatest challenge facing the human race*. In one form or another, priests and rabbis and theologians and philosophers have wrestled with the problem for thousands of years. Unfortunately, their answers always leave us wondering what was left out.

For us who believe in and love God, we find that to lash our consciences and stir up feelings of guilt over our difficulties in "getting along" is counterproductive, for it sometimes exacerbates the situation. We simply cannot evade the biblical truth: The planet is under a curse. Evil powers are working steadily in our midst, seeking to destroy the human race. How else can we account for Hitler, Stalin, and all the cruelties of the twentieth century? As General Douglas MacArthur truly remarked aboard the USS *Missouri* at the end of World War II, the answer is "theological." But to say that alone is hardly enough.

Meanwhile the man in the street has come up with his own answer. He says if there is a God, and He is good, then He obviously cannot smile at the behavior of the human race. In fact, He must be grinding His teeth and exhibiting wrath at the way we treat each other. But since so much human behavior today is still perfidious, God must lack the power to correct it; therefore He cannot be almighty. And if He does have the power to correct but fails to use it, then He can hardly be called "good."

This street-smart reasoning leaves millions of humans bewildered as to whom and what they should worship. Many well-fed North Americans may be naturally inclined to think of God as good. They cannot understand why tragic things happen, and they don't think anyone else knows why either. Apart from the problem of their own sinful natures, there is the problem of the devil. Examining the nature of evil is to them an unpleasant task. It is looking down into a long, dark, sinister tunnel.

The gospel response to the problem of evil in the world is simple. It is *faith in Jesus Christ and trust in God*. When Jesus went to the cross to die for our sins (on our behalf and in our stead), He lifted the curse of sin from us who love Him, and bore it Himself. His shed blood took away our wrongdoings, our guilt, and our punishment forever.

"Gone, gone, gone, gone, all our sins are gone!"

JOY—EVEN WITHOUT ALL THE ANSWERS

Today we who believe that God is good have learned to trust Him implicitly, even when we don't understand and when our reason is tested, puzzled, and at times frustrated. The apostle Paul himself spoke of "the mystery of iniquity."[2] Honesty requires that we admit we don't have all the answers and that we certainly can't "explain" what is going on in heaven. I mean, we just don't know—but we recall the words of the Lord to Isaiah: "My thoughts are not your thoughts, neither are your ways my ways."[3] So we clam up, keep quiet, and trust God.

Sometimes this gets funny. Once, when driving through the California desert, I came upon a fancy castle built by an old prospector named "Death Valley Scotty." In front of this ornate building a sign is erected that carries a few of his original sayings. I have never forgotten them. They read,

> Don't say nothing bad about anybody.
> Don't give advice.
> Don't explain.
> Don't complain.

What Scotty seems to be implying is, when you can't "explain," don't. Apply it to us Christians and it makes some sense. Many an unbeliever won't accept our "explanation" of the gospel, and a believer doesn't need it. A similar saying that appealed to me appeared years ago in a Bronx comic strip. An old Yiddish-speaking housewife was answering everybody's questions with two words:

"Dunt esk!"

Such advice at least keeps us wondering. Some day "the silver cord will be loosed and the golden bowl be broken," and the answers will come, glorious and lucid. How do we know they will? By faith, and faith alone. Jesus told us, "In that day you will ask Me nothing. Whatever you ask the Father in My name He will give you."[4]

In biblical times people often found social conditions dismal in the extreme, and today we find outrageous things still with us, things bombarding us hourly through our television screens. With all our expanding resources we have failed appallingly to create a truly peaceful environment, whether it be on a continent or an island of the sea. The reason? A willful breakdown in our personal relationships.

For 17 years I saw this, as part of the team of one of the most fascinating men of recent history, the Reverend William Franklin Graham. As his editor, I was privileged to travel with him to all six inhabited continents and the islands of the sea. He knew his world, and he observed to us more than once that all the current conflicts between human groupings are actually religious wars.

Whether it be Northern Irish Protestant versus Southern Irish Catholic, or Indian Hindu and Sikh versus Pakistani Muslim, or Jew versus Muslim in Palestine, or Quebecois Roman Catholic against Canadian Protestant, or Northern Nigerian Muslim against Southern Nigerian Christian, or Chinese Communism against Christian faith, or Serbian Orthodox against Kosovo Muslim, *the hostility invariably has a religious origin and base.* All these people are really arguing, quarreling, fighting, and killing each other about God!

And what does God do when the nations rage "furiously together" and the people "plot a vain thing?"[5] The psalmist tells us: "He who sits in the heavens shall laugh."[6] Divine derision!

I found it fascinating to watch Billy Graham make his way amiably through so many of these intense rivalries and secular and religious groupings that have plagued the twentieth, and now the twenty-first centuries. Invariably his approach has been pleasant, gentlemanly, uncritical, Spirit-filled and cloaked in the love of Jesus. As a result, I saw him welcomed as a holy man wherever he went. (Only the now-discredited Communists and an opportunistic biographer or two still criticize him openly.) Even in his eighties Billy remains a servant of the Most High God and of Jesus Christ, His Son, no matter what the religious tradition of those he visited. He has left his mark on the world. The world almost likes him, and the church loves him.[*]

Like Billy Graham, we can do something better than stew, chew, and puzzle over the "mystery of iniquity" in the world.

---

[*] At the present writing Dr. and Mrs. Graham need much prayer. Neither of them is in good health. Nevertheless she continues her writing ministry, and he continues to minister around the world, proclaiming the gospel to vast crowds, loving people everywhere and being loved by them.

The gospel teaches us that instead of looking down into that dark evil tunnel, we should *look up*. And *keep* looking up. Even physically! J.I. Packer tells us, "The most universally awesome experience that mankind knows is to stand alone on a clear night and look at the stars."[7] I keep a five-foot telescope in my study. I know that behind all the nebulae, stars, planets, and asteroids I can see through that telescope is the great Lord God Himself, and I contend He hasn't stopped smiling. In the Holy Bible He has told us that He loves you and me, and has shown us by His Spirit that His way is still the right way and the only way, and that it is open to us all.

And what is that way? It is the way of love. Just as the sun comes up every morning, so every day is a new day for our heavenly Father to extend his warm hand of love to the humanity He created. In our response, we can reach out with one hand to take His, and with the other hand we can reach out to each other.

"Love God and love your neighbor" is, in a way, the ultimate aim and message of Christianity. We can will to conduct ourselves in ways that please God by loving each other, respecting each other, helping each other, encouraging each other, praying for each other, being kind and generous toward each other, working with each other for the good of the whole, and having fun with each other.

The stars are still shining.

Our God is still smiling.

GOD'S PEOPLE REJOICE IN HIM

9
GOD SMILES ON RADIANT LOVE

Let him kiss me with the kisses of his mouth.
—SONG OF SONGS 1:2

*L*ike a velvet-covered case that a secret spring snaps open, this alluring invitation begins the most beautiful and controversial book of the Holy Bible, the Song of Songs (which, by the way, is the original Hebrew title).

The verse quoted above is the only reference in the 66 books of the Bible to a man and a woman joining in a kiss. And the magnificent Song of Songs is itself one of the few surviving books of the ancient world, as far as I know, in which a godly woman seems completely and gloriously free to be herself. It is also the most famous and the most popular love poem ever written.

Someone asked a famous English literary critic, George E.B. Saintsbury (1845–1933), to name his choice as the finest passage in the whole range of English literature. He immediately responded by selecting a passage in the Song of Songs, King James Version:

> Set me as a seal upon thine heart,
> as a seal upon thine arm:
> for love is strong as death;
> …many waters cannot quench love,
> neither can the floods drown it (8:6,7).

As this lovely poem shows us so vividly, the Creator God gave us love to enhance the joy of living and to add fragrance and meaning to the ongoing propagation of the race. Whether it be family love, friendly love, or humane or benevolent love, they are all part of God's gift of love, which comes to us wreathed in smiles. Is this gift still with us today in our new millennium? Absolutely! Let me show you how it works. Our illustration will reflect the basic relationship: love between a man and a woman.

The immediate scene before us is the twenty-first-century home, such as it is, occupied by a legally married man and woman, such as they are. God Himself graciously provided a lawful ordinance to protect this conventional kind of married love. No sprucing up. No false hair. No photo ops. As Sancho Panza once said, "We are all as God made us, and oftentimes a great deal worse!"[1]

Because I have spent 60 years wrapped in the gentle bonds of matrimony and am still enjoying it, I choose to enter the discussion of this subject myself. My experience as a marriage counselor does not go beyond that of the average minister. Still, over six decades one tends to learn what works and what doesn't work.

Having been faithful to my marriage vows, I sense the warmth of God's smile on that sacred ordinance. I understand why He in His Word chose to make the love and joy of holy matrimony the image of Christ and His church. The Bible describes Jesus as the heavenly Bridegroom, whose sacred relationship to His earthbound followers (His church) is sealed by the celestial marriage of the Bridegroom to His bride. Thus not only does the Son of God come to His church as Savior and Lord, but by this beautiful figure God links the institution of marriage to His beloved gospel of salvation.

Let me assure my readers who happen to be single that a later chapter will fully and gladly consider the wider bounds of Christian friendship and love beyond that of matrimony. Right now we shall take a moment out of the new millennium to explore the hallowed state of *nuptiae delectae,* the garden of married delights.

The chosen scene will be the dining area at Chez Wirt on a weekday morning. After prayer and breakfast, I inform my wife that I have typed a letter and will drive to the post office to mail it. Ruth suggests that I could put it in our own mailbox and it would be picked up. But since I am going to the post office, would I mind purchasing some stamps and mailing some packages to the children and grandchildren?

Then there are some clothes to be picked up at the cleaners, and developed photos to be retrieved at the camera shop, and we need money, so hadn't I better stop at the bank? By the way, our milk supply is low, and would I mind driving her car as it needs gas? And while I am out, why don't I get a haircut? For her part, she has a big washing to do and bulbs to plant, an older neighbor to visit, and the cat needs to go to the vet. Do I argue or protest at all the running about? What good will it do? Besides, I love it. There is joy in our home. We put each other first.

Not only am I a married man, I am a sports lover. As a sports editor I used to appreciate the remark of William Lyon Phelps, a revered teacher of English literature at Yale University, who said, "I read the front page of the newspaper every day to learn about man's failures. Then I turn to the sports page to learn about his successes."

Now I am going to make my wedded masculine readers a sporting proposition. Here is the challenge. I assume that a working biblical relationship exists between you and God. That being the case, just for sport, mind you, I'm suggesting that you consider putting your wife at the top of your list *in everything* for one week, starting today. She is *"it."* No exceptions, no reservations. Just establish her there at the apex of your life and keep her there during waking hours for seven days. Don't tell her what's going on. On my part, I promise no rewards. Just see what happens.

> *My lover is mine and I am his;*
> *He browses among the lilies.*
> —SONG OF SONGS 2:16 NIV

Let me tell you about a woman I know. She is now happily married, but an earlier union linked her to a schoolteacher, and after the first year she left him. When I asked why, she told me, "I became Number Four."

When I pressed for an explanation, she explained, "To my husband his father rated Number One. After school each day he went to see Dad. The beach rated Number Two. My husband was a part-time lifeguard, and whenever he could, he headed for the beach crowd, as he loved the environment and its camaraderie. Number Three was his big dog. They went everywhere together. That meant in his life I was Number Four."

> *I opened for my lover,*
> *But my lover had left; he was gone.*
> —5:6 NIV

I have been around long enough to see homes on every continent where the wife is Number Two, or Three, or whatever. The car comes first, or the fishing rod, or another member of the family, or the golf partner, or the workplace, or (God help us) the church. No wonder there are problems—by the dumpsterful. Often have I felt like interfering with, "*She is your wife, man! Your consort, your soul mate!*"

If that schoolteacher husband had studied Scripture, particularly the book of Proverbs, the Song of Songs, the Gospels, and Paul's letters to the Ephesians and Philippians, he would not have put his dog ahead of the queen of his heart. He would have realized that the Bible has a very high view of the wife in any family. She is the mistress of the household, the lady of the hearth, not part of the chattel.

It's true that the wife is called a "helpmeet," and that is certainly her role, but not exclusively by any means. Her "help" in any case leans on where her relationship with her husband stands. If she has locked-in that assurance she ranks *right at the top* in his world view—no problem. She will be there to help if she can, and he is a fortunate man. He has a devoted wife. God is smiling on him.

> *How delightful is your love, my sister, my bride!*
> *How much more pleasing is your love than wine.*
> —4:10 NIV

Experience has taught me that no responsibility we undertake in life ranks above the relationship with our marriage partner. Under God no task, no job, no assignment, no church, no club, no obligation comes before the person we choose to marry. That includes the beloved children of the household and the honored parents and in-laws. Remember, children grow up and leave home; parents eventually retreat into retirement; but our spouse stays, and stays, and stays, thank God.

Since this arrangement is scriptural, God honors it. When the family sees that a spouse respects and honors his or her mate, when friends and neighbors and fellow workers observe the mutual commitment, then the real romance flourishes like orange blossoms. Then the fun begins and benefits accrue. Incidentally, endearing love between husband and wife provides invaluable insurance that the whole family is secure.

You have ravished my heart,
My sister, my spouse;
You have ravished my heart
With one look of your eyes,
With one link of your necklace.
—4:9

No man expects his wife to take over and run his life, or vice versa. As for the husband, the Bible teaches that you are to love your wife as Christ loved the church. And how did Christ love the church? Christ died for the church.[2]

When we put our spouse first, we may feel a bit awkward. What am I doing? What's the point of it? Even your wife or husband wonders what is going on. Yet it is amazing when we do it how things seem to solve themselves. When an offer—any offer—comes to you, bring her or him into it. "We're a team!" If eyebrows go up, let 'em go up. Your marriage is more important, and this attitude will uplift you both. When I am asked to travel, as on a book tour, I ask automatically, "What about Ruth?" She goes along. It makes for an exciting marriage.

Now a word to the married woman. A wife's role is usually the key to any family's success. There are times, encumbered by family emergencies, when she must put first things first—not necessarily her husband. He should be the first to agree. No problem. Blessed are the flexible! So he politely dances out of the way but comes back strong. Why not? There are no waves. God's yoke is easy, as Jesus taught.

But the Word of God also teaches that in the long run, the priorities remain—her husband comes first after God, and that is the way to a successful and radiant marital relationship, with peace of mind, security, fulfillment, and above all, love.

What? You don't believe it? You think it will make things worse? Try it.

Gaye Wheat writes,

> To serve one's husband for Jesus' sake does not
> demand that one be servile and abject as with a
> Babylonian slave or an eighteenth-century washer-
> woman. It begins with the attitude of thinking about
> him, instead of being preoccupied with myself. The
> behavior that pleases him flows out of an inner attitude
> that I have already chosen for myself—the attitude
> that my husband is the king of my household and the
> king of my marriage. He is my top priority, right after
> Christ. So it is my joy and privilege to treat my hus-
> band as my lord.[3]

> *How beautiful you are, my darling,*
> *Oh, how beautiful!*
> *...There is no flaw in you*
> *...The fragrance of your garments*
> *Is like that of Lebanon.*
> —4:1,7,11 NIV

What about meeting her husband halfway? Isn't that enough?
Won't it show that a wife is accommodating herself to his
choices, his desires, his career? Shouldn't a wife, as Ruth
Graham puts it, "fit into her husband's plans"? Doesn't the Bible
itself say that to be a good wife, she is to do certain things?

Here I must walk very carefully, for I don't wish to seem to
encourage the wrong things. The halfway commitment? Don't
count on it too much. The Christian wife reads her Bible. She
knows what it says about submission. She knows the score. But
at the moment she may not be looking to Peter or Paul, she may
be looking to her husband for guidelines as to how she should
behave toward him. She is waiting to see who he really is by his
attitude toward her. There is no trade-off here, no balancing act.

We are assuming that with her, he, her husband, comes first after God. But how, after God, does she rank with him? Does he act as if she comes first?

Handsome is as handsome does. In George Bernard Shaw's play *Pygmalion,* Professor Henry Higgins, a priggish philologist, is educated by a flower girl from the east side of London, Miss Eliza Doolittle. She tells him, "The difference between a lady and a flower girl is not how she behaves, but how she is treated."[4]

Assuming a husband does put his wife first after God, what is the return for all his adulation? What's his takeaway from a marriage that is truly a marriage of love?

Well, if his wife really does come first after God, then she quickly becomes the most important person on earth to him. She becomes his soul mate, his better half, his best friend, his life partner, his intimate lover, his passport to joy. The marriage is working.

Un moment, mesdames, take note of the phrase, "She becomes his passport to joy." Try linking that expression with Gilbert Chesterton's ingenious remark, "Man is more himself, is more manlike, *when joy is the fundamental thing in him.*"

Ladies and gentlemen, have fun.

> *Let my lover come into his garden*
> *And taste its choice fruits.*
> —4:16 NIV

So what about the wife's responsibility as a mother and as a daughter? First, what about bringing up her children as Christian believers and good citizens to serve God and maintain the social order? Is she not expected to "look after the kids"? Of course she is, but so is her husband; and the best way to do that is to secure the stability of the family through the relationship of husband and wife. Then the wife has her husband's participation in child-rearing. God uses fathers as well as mothers in the propagation and rearing of the human species.

Then what about obligations owed to the parents on both sides of the family? Suppose the relationship is hurting because one or more parents objected to the marriage in the first place. I believe when they see their children are really happy and have found a congenial church, parents are more likely to be satisfied with the marriage relationship. Also, a husband will not quickly develop hostility with his in-laws if he sees their daughter radiating joy in his home.

Finally, how does all this work out in practice? For many centuries, happily married people would not discuss their marriages publicly. Modesty and the "sanctity of the home" prevented it. Today this has changed socially somewhat, and it's not all for the worse. For example, many excellent books on sex and marriage are now available in Christian bookstores to help believing life-partners. Ruth and I particularly recommend books by Ed and Gaye Wheat, Clifford and Joyce Penner, and Tim and Beverly LaHaye.[5]

We live in a commercial world that views sex as a prime commodity to exploit for profit. Unless we Christians recognize this, we are in big trouble. A pair of women's legs will sell a set of tires or a birdhouse. The fabricated lie prevails over the truth. The followers of postmodern thinking assure us that no absolutes exist; that everything is relative.

Husbands and boyfriends accordingly adopt such a lifestyle and choose to be aggressive and brutal. They try to humiliate others, to put themselves first, and generally they seek to order their women around. So treated, women either bow out, fight back, or turn into complainers and join the dreary chorus of the dissatisfied millions. As a result, both husband and wife lose the smile of heaven and spoil the most beautiful gift God ever gave to men and women.

There's a way out of the trash heap, a golden path. If you forget everything else I have written in this chapter, remember my sporting challenge, and these words: Under God, **put your spouse first.**

> *Make haste, my beloved,*
> *And be like a gazelle*
> *Or a young stag*
> *On the mountains of spices.*
> —8:14

10

GOD SMILES ON CHILDREN

❧

He who gives a child a treat
Makes joy-bells ring in Heaven's street.

—JOHN MASEFIELD

I was in Guadalajara, Mexico," my friend Gary Priest, an assistant curator at the famous San Diego Zoo, told me, "and I was giving llama rides to a group of children aged three to twelve, when one little girl caught my eye. She had big brown eyes and a winning smile, and seemed to stand out from the crowd. She stood there alone. As I lifted her onto the llama's back, she never said a word, but once under way, I saw her expression become one of unbridled joy. In fact, her look put a bounce in my own step.

"At the end of the ride I lifted her off the llama and the little girl started to walk away. Then she stopped, turned back, and gently tapped at my leg. She motioned for me to bend down, as though she would whisper to me. Then unexpectedly she pecked a thank-you kiss on my cheek. Tears still well up in my eyes as I think about that special moment when God smiled on us. It was a rare kind of joy, such as I had when I understood what it was to accept my heavenly Father's gift of love and eternal life."

Do you think God loves children? He adores them! They're His precious darlings. In some ways they are His joyous masterpieces of Creation. That may become clearer when we examine the New Testament, where Jesus' contacts with children were so loving, gentle, and life-affirming. As a consequence, Jesus has been winning the hearts of human beings ever since. People of every age and race and color and tongue have put their confidence in His gospel, and so have validated His truth.

I love kids. As a pastor I loved telling children's stories from the pulpit. When serving as editor of Billy Graham's magazine, *Decision,* I would go to the mail room and dig out children's letters to Billy and publish them. Invariably they were both charming and deeply spiritual. Children (especially our two splendid grandchildren!) amaze me with their perception of reality and their discernment of falsity. God often gives children great insights into life.

GOD'S SMILE IS ON THE FAMILY

I know God created children to love and serve Him, but He also invented them for our grown-up delight as well. His organic plan to populate the earth has become our greatest human source of joy.

> Start them small and grow them big,
> Slow but sure and rig-a-jig-jig.

That's for the kids. Give them parents to guide them but not to control them, to inspire them but not to coddle them. Oh, yes, kids can be rascals and even criminals. To label them innocent is to go against Scripture and to belie truth. But there is hope for each and every one of them.

Specialists of our postmodern era are now tinkering with childbirth—childbirth in ways other than normal—just as they are tinkering with ways to reach the surface of other planets. If they would only ask God, they would learn that their experiments will in time prove unproductive. Life is mysterious. God is mysterious. To draw a contrast, some of the early astronauts were aware of the supernatural risks involved in their space trips to the moon, so they read aloud the book of Genesis in mid-flight. Good thinking! I urge all frozen-sperm specialists now in mid-experiment to forget the market for the moment and ask for divine advice about ways to bring children into the world, before it is too late.

From the beginning God has smiled on the human family, which by definition includes children. God has given us His counsel in a well-known proverb: "Train up a child in the way he should go, and when he is old he will not depart from it."[1] Is there a right way in life, and a wrong way? The Bible is clear. God told the prophet Jeremiah, "Thus says the LORD: Stand in the ways and see, and ask for the old paths, where the good way is, and walk in it; then you will find rest for your souls."[2] That's the surest route.

OUR SAVIOR WAS A CHILD

Our television screens portrayed for us a fascinating sight on January 1, 2000, when cities around the world staged dazzling outdoor shows to welcome the New Year and the New Millennium. From Paris to Sydney to Nairobi the lights and fireworks lit up the sky. Nothing like this celebration had ever occurred in human history. Everybody loved it.

Yet it was one of the great *faux-pas* of all time. Almost all the cities ignored the Person whose birthday party it was. They were unconsciously celebrating the two-thousandth birthday of Jesus of Nazareth. One or two cities did notice that this was an honor paid to the Christchild, born (approximately) in A.D. 1, but all the great crowds acted as if they were completely unaware of it. So why celebrate? All that really happened was a change in numbers: 1999 to 2000. But 2000 what? Beans? Peanuts? Ostrich eggs? Pizzas?

It was 2000 years ago that God Himself undertook to stage a show—a show to celebrate the birth of His baby Son. And He did it in a way that could have put the Eiffel Tower and Sydney Harbor Bridge in the dark, so to speak. Twenty centuries ago Hebrew shepherds on watch outside the village of Bethlehem in Palestine saw an electric show that lighted up the surrounding fields with dazzling brilliance. And here's an odd thing—people ever since that day have been reading about it on Bible scrolls and in books, and have been talking about it. How far into the future do you think we will be reading about those Y2K celebrations?

Let me remind you of this different birthday party.

About the year 1 (A.D.), some royal astrologers, seeking to worship a newborn king, followed a new moving star that led them across the Mesopotamian desert from Persia to Judea. They believed it signified the birth of a baby, a newborn king, and they desired to worship Him. Ultimately the star directed them to Bethlehem. There angels appeared to shepherds in the fields, uttering expressions of joy. Were they singing? How could they help but sing? Mary herself had sung earlier when she learned of her pregnancy: "My soul magnifies the Lord, and my spirit has rejoiced in God my Savior."[3]

According to the Bible, with the glory of the Lord shining around him, an angel spoke to the shepherds: "I bring you good tidings of great joy which will be to all people. For there is born to you this day in the city of David a Savior, who is Christ the Lord."[4] Then joining the angel came a "multitude of the heavenly host, praising God." The wise men and the shepherds, the rich and the poor, came to Bethlehem, found Jesus, and worshiped. Afterward the astrologer-kings went back to their homes, and the shepherds went, not to church (as Luther pointed out), but back to the world's work. Quickly and widely the word spread: God had smiled upon His Son Jesus, a child of Israel, and through Him upon the whole world.

About Jesus' early childhood almost nothing is known, apart from His proper obedience to Joseph and Mary. Later some hacks would fabricate imaginary stories, but they were soon exposed as fallacious. We are compensated for the absence of genuine records of Jesus' growing up, I believe, by what we read of our Lord's adult attitude toward children. The tenderness He manifested in His contacts with children during His ministry tells us that Jesus must have had pleasurable memories of His own childhood. The one picture we have, of the 12-year-old Jesus talking with the elders in the temple in Jerusalem, tells us even more.[5] It speaks of boldness of spirit, of sharpness of mind, and of deep and special love for His Father in heaven. Already Jesus had a prescient consciousness of His future; yet as time went on, He never forgot that He, too, was once a little child.

When during His Galilean ministry sick and dying children were brought to Him, Jesus' loving touch restored them to life and to their parents. He left a legacy so strong in its link to children that today, 2000 years later, the church of Christ is still following its Founder by carrying on a faithful ministry to children of all ages. During long periods of history and even today, when children everywhere in the world are still neglected, exploited, and sold into sin and slavery, the church of God has kept the faith and has not forgotten to minister to its little ones.

CHILDREN ARE THE LORD'S

When it became apparent that my late wife, Winola, and I would have no children of our own, a handsome little 3-year-old moved into our house. God had smiled on us and had given us this Scottish laddie named Alexander, but called by the Scots "Wee Eck." And what an endearing son Alexander Wells Wirt has been and what a joyful experience fatherhood became to me! But what a mountainous responsibility! Society had placed this little boy in our hands with unspoken, silent, unwritten orders to take care of him. But to us it involved more than society, for God had also done the same; and His orders were written plainly in His own Book.

It made me smile with pride when our new son came home from Sunday School repeating the verses of Proverbs 3:5,6 (KJV):

> Trust in the LORD with all thine heart; and lean not
> unto thine own understanding. In all thy ways
> acknowledge him, and he shall direct thy paths.

When 21-year-old Alex came home from Vietnam with four Purple Heart medals, I was more sure than ever that God was "directing his paths."

Our son was a rich blessing to our home, but some parents today are wondering whether God is smiling on their children. For some people, the proverbial joys of childhood have turned into nightmares, since in today's twenty-first century the rearing of children has become more difficult than ever. No subject is more heatedly discussed in every American forum, along with its many ramifications; and the problems keep mounting until the proverbial joys of childhood are becoming rare. Some parents are beginning to fear their children. Young couples are quietly choosing to "skip the kid bit."

In dealing with family crises as a pastor, I have learned over and over in life never to sell God short. His righteousness always comes through and wins the day, while we fuss and sputter and drop like apricots in June. Just when we have about given up in hopelessness, a new solution appears. A new face appears on the landscape, a new body to strike a blow for truth, purity, and integrity. How it happens may appear a mystery, but God knows. A friend of ours, Norman Pell of Melbourne,

Australia, likes to say, "I never know whether God is guiding my decisions or overruling my mistakes!" The point is, God is at work.

We do know that God is not deaf. He reigns, He listens. He will survive Century XXI whatever it brings. New Nietzsches will deny Him, new drug lords will appear, and new pornographers will clutter the internet, seeking to destroy the soul of humanity. They will all fail. God will continue to win good children away from dissolute parents and rescue good parents from their own dissolute progeny through the washing of regeneration and the renewing of the Holy Spirit.[6]

I have now reached an age when I am certain that God is not frowning on our children and grandchildren—He is smiling on them. He loves them. If they have not already done so, He wants them to come into His kingdom, to join those lining up for the march before His throne.

New leaders will replace tyrants. By His Holy Spirit, our smiling God will continue to pour genuine spiritual revival into the life of the church. With a renewed proclamation of the glad tidings of the gospel of Jesus Christ, the church will again find its true role. It will teach little children who will listen, learn, clap, sing, pray, and even lead their own parents into the eternal temple of God's truth.

11
GOD SMILES WHEN WE COME TO HIM

❧

Betwixt the stirrup and the ground
Mercy I asked, mercy I found.

—WILLIAM CAMDEN (1551–1623)

*M*illions of people have received and known salvation in Christ. Millions of others have not. What does it mean? How does it happen?

Being saved can occur in a flash, in a minute, in an hour, in a day, or it can be spread over a longer period; but when it takes place, it is very, very real. It can seem like leaving the earth and coming back. Or being transported suddenly to ancient Palestine. It is entirely the work of the Holy Spirit. Convicted by the Spirit, we open our hearts to the Lord Jesus Christ and receive Him as Redeemer and Master in a resolute abandonment and capitulation of self.

Salvation is a work of God, for God, by God. As the old King James version quaintly renders the apostle Paul's words, "So then it is not of him that willeth, nor of him that runneth, but of God that sheweth mercy."[1] It comes with joy, but the joy we feel is not like any other joy. It is a fruit of the Holy Spirit, and its effect on us is something like a second birthday. It makes us want to celebrate. That is our human response to the grace and goodness of Almighty God.

Salvation in Christ can approach us quietly, with a feeling of peace and relief. It can come with a shower of tears or a

87

shout of rapture and ecstasy, or with a rueful shaking of the
head or a slump of surrender. It can come in a dying moment.
It can come in a moment of revival. It can come with a cry of
thanksgiving for healing or with a quick dash to find and tell
someone. A thousand new saints may adopt a thousand different responses to a smiling God, but they all signify the same
thing—SAVED! SAVED!

And they all bring joy to the hosts of heaven, for Jesus said
"There is joy in the presence of the angels of God over one
sinner who repents"![2]

Perhaps the best way to describe the joyful response of the
new creatures in Christ is to hear their own descriptive testimonies. I have borrowed and assembled a few stories out of
the millions in God's own collection. Some of the following
are from well-known people, some are from people unknown
except to the Lord Himself.

CLIVE STAPLES LEWIS (1898–1963)

On September 28, 1931, C.S. Lewis traveled from The Kilns, his home just outside of Oxford, England, to Whipsnade Zoo in the sidecar of his brother Warren's motorcycle. He wrote later that on that short trip his conversion to Christ became a reality. As he described it, "When we set out I did not believe that Jesus Christ is the Son of God, and when we reached the zoo I did."

Thirty years later, in an interview with Mr. Lewis for *Decision* magazine at his quarters in Magdalen College, Cambridge University, I asked him, "Do you feel that you made a decision at the time of your conversion?"

His reply was, "I feel my decision was not so important. I was the object rather than the subject in this affair. *I was decided upon*. At the moment what I heard was God saying, 'Put down your gun and we'll talk.' "[3]

WANDA JONES

Gracious, well-loved teacher, wife of evangelist Howard Jones of the Billy Graham team, mother of five children and six grandchildren.

My mother had a wonderful faith. My earliest memories are of playing with my dolls and hearing her in the bedroom, where she would be kneeling beside her bed, praying and sometimes weeping for the salvation of each of her nine children. My father being also a Christian, cottage prayer meetings met regularly in our home.

When I reached twelve years of age my mother died. I lost interest in school, and a great emptiness took over my life. Five years later I attended my parents' church to hear some young men who called themselves the "Biola Trumpeters." On the closing night of their appearance they impressed me tremendously with their sincerity. Obviously they *enjoyed* being Christians. After playing, they gave their testimonies and told us they knew their sins were forgiven.

When they gave an invitation to come forward to receive Christ, I went. About fifteen other young people made the same response. The lady pastor prayed with us and *I felt a sense of great peace and inner joy.* For the first time since my mother's death, God filled the void in my life. I knew that Christ had come into my heart, that I had experienced the new birth I had heard so much about. My mother's prayers for me had been answered.[4]

SAUL KANE

I know the very words I said,
They bayed like bloodhounds in my head;
"All God's bells will carol soon
For joy and glory and delight
Of someone coming home tonight."
Out into darkness, out to night,
My flaring heart gave plenty light...
And in my heart the drink unpriced,
The burning cataracts of Christ.
I did not think, I did not strive,
The deep peace burnt my me alive;
The bolted door had broken in,
I knew that I had done with sin.
The waters rushing from the rain
Were singing Christ has risen again.
O glory of the lighted mind.
How dead I'd been, how dumb, how blind!
I thought all earthly creatures knelt
From rapture of the joy I felt.

—from "The Everlasting Mercy," John Masefield[5]

BILL STILES

Bill Stiles, one of the last members of the Jesse James gang, was planning another train robbery in 1913. On the day before the "hit," as he walked on Los Angeles' Main Street, he saw a policeman coming toward him and ducked into the Union Rescue Mission nearby. To avoid being followed, he walked clear to the front and sat down.

He said later, "I did not hear much of the service, for my mind was upon the work for the next day. I felt a little uneasy, for I had left my suitcase in my room, and in it some of the 'soup' (nitroglycerine), some high explosives, and my guns. I was just getting up to leave the mission when one worker came to me and asked me to give myself up to God.

"I told him that I did not believe in a God. I don't remember his reply, for when I attempted to get up I had no control over my legs. They were fastened to that floor by a power not of this earth. A woman came and sat down beside me and urged me to go up to the altar. I listened to her for a time and consented to go, thinking it would do me no harm. As soon as I gave my consent my legs were released and I went up and knelt at the altar.

"I heard them praying and a strange feeling came over me. It seemed as though something on my heart was loosening up, and *I began to feel happy.* How sorry I began to feel for my past life of crime. I could not keep back the tears—tears of real repentance. I heard them tell me to repeat a prayer, but I had found the Lord before that. *Oh, what a joy came into my heart!*"[6]

AN UNKNOWN GIRL

Nothing, humanly speaking, could be done for the young woman at the hospital. She had come in an ambulance from a disreputable part of a large city where she had been stabbed in a drunken brawl. A nurse sat beside her, waiting till the end would come.

There were coarse lines in the youthful face. Presently she opened her eyes and spoke: "I want you to tell me something and tell me straight," she addressed the nurse. "Do you think God cares about people like me? Do you think He could forgive anyone as bad as me?"

At first the nurse didn't dare to answer until, to use the Quaker John Woolman's expression, she had "turned her mind inwardly to the Lord." Then she reached out to this needy girl and felt a sense of oneness. *She offered a radiant and authoritative testimony:* "I'm telling you straight: God cares about you, and He forgives you."

A new gentleness and beauty appeared on the face of the girl as she slipped back into unconsciousness. The nurse had the privilege that day of witnessing to the love of Christ to [one who was] dying.[7]

FESTO KIVENGERE (1920–1988)

World-famous evangelist, bishop of the Anglican Church of Uganda, born and brought up in Africa, educated in Church Missionary Society schools, he barely escaped execution by the former dictator of Uganda, then authored a book titled *I Love Idi Amin*. A product of the East African revival, Festo was a truly saintly man, greatly beloved.

> One Sunday afternoon in Kabale I was coming home from a drinking party to which I had intentionally gone because one of these *balokole* ("saved ones") had witnessed that I was going to be converted that day. I wanted to drink exceptionally hard so that it would be impossible for me to be converted.
>
> As I was returning, I met a fellow schoolmaster who had found Jesus Christ during a church service just three hours before. Three hours, no more, he had been a Christian when he stopped me. He looked me full in the face and said, "When you left me in the church, I found Jesus and He is in my heart. I want to talk over the things I have said contrary to Christ."
>
> The Lord used that special testimony to turn me completely around. I arrived home in utter misery. I knelt by my bed for the first time, and this is what I remember saying to God:
>
> "God, if you are there, and if Christ actually died for sinners like me, and if He can change me as I have seen others changed, and if the Bible is not a mere story book cooked up by Europeans to deceive us, here I am; save me. I know I am a sinner. I know the judgment for sin is over me. Here is my heart. I accept the finished sacrifice of Christ on Calvary."

The next moment was wonderful. My burden had fallen off. Judgment was gone. I saw, as it were, my name written over Christ's on the cross. I went outside my house a liberated man and began giving my testimony, and I have never been the same since.[8]

WESLEY H. DICKENS

I am an organist. For 15 nights during the summer of 1957 I attended the Billy Graham Crusade in Madison Square Garden, New York City. I avoided going forward to be saved. If my friends went forward, I would accompany them and explain to the counselor, "I am a Christian," which I wasn't. Later I learned that these same friends were praying for me.

On Saturday night, July 13, the evangelist's voice boomed out, "One thing thou lackest." We were sitting in the balcony, three girls from our church and myself, and his words reverberated in my heart. I wanted to go up with the hundreds who were responding at the time of the invitation, and turned to the girls. "Don't any of you want to go up?"

"No."

Well, I thought, *I can come alone tomorrow night and give my life to Christ then.* (Thus Satan reasoned with my heart.) After a time the choir stopped singing. "Thank God," I said. "It's too late now. It's got to be tomorrow night." I settled back, but could not relax. The text kept hounding me, "One thing thou lackest."

"Wait! I'm sorry, but there's something I must do." Billy Graham had moved to the microphone once more. "I've never done this before," he explained, "but I won't feel at peace tonight unless I do it. I have the feeling there is one person out in the audience who ought to be up here."

I wasn't prepared for this.

"That person needs Christ tonight. He's gripping his seat to keep from coming." A dreadful silence ensued. I looked down at my hands. They were clamped so tightly around the chair that my knuckles were white. I let go so suddenly I nearly slid onto the floor.

Billy Graham's voice rose excitedly. "I think it's a young man out there, in the balcony!" Then I began to shake. "He thinks he can come another night." He pointed his finger into the balcony at me and said, "I want to tell you something, young man, whoever you are. You can't come to Christ when you want to. You can come only when the Spirit of God is drawing you." More quietly he added, "I'm going to ask the choir to sing one verse of 'Almost Persuaded' while you come."

That was all I could take. Turning to the girls I asked again, "Don't any of you want to go forward?" They shook their heads. "Well, then, you'll have to excuse me, because I've got to." I turned and leaped out of my seat. Head swimming, knees shaking, but *with joy in my heart,* I made it to the escalator. Not another person moved in that great building as I ran toward the rostrum. Thousands on every side, but I no longer cared. I thought, *I'm coming, Lord Christ!*

That night I returned to my room, knowing one thing only: *I'm saved.* Yes, saved, here and now, and forever! Praise the Lord.[9]

12

WHEN SMILING LEADS TO LAUGHTER

✇

*I have never known why it should
be considered derogatory to the Creator to
suppose that He has a sense of humor.*

—DEAN WILLIAM R. INGE, ST. PAUL'S, LONDON

*A*rchbishop William Temple used to tell the story of an Englishman in Ireland who asked a local citizen the way to the town of Roscommon. "Is it Roscommon you're wantin' to go to?" asked the Irishman.

"Yes," said the Englishman, "that's why I asked the way."

"Well," said the Irishman, "if I wanted to go to Roscommon, I wouldn't be startin' from here."[1]

The Archbishop's Irishman spoke well. From "here" you can't get to Roscommon, and you can't get to the Joy of the Lord either. So perhaps the best way for us to start looking for that joy is to laugh. The very idea of such a search is ridiculous. But then, so are we; and when we realize it, the laugh itself becomes a breakthrough. Philip Yancey, after visiting churches around the world, was left with the impression that "not many people in church look as if they're enjoying themselves." What an indictment! It isn't always that we are sad, we just *look* sad. And as long as we are such solemn critters, we won't get far with real New Testament joy.

If you object to our search for laughter and say there is nothing humorous in the Bible, let me remind you of Jesus' description of a camel trying to go through a needle's eye. As a further example, one of Jesus' parables has had the theological world in a dizzy spin ever since He told it. In Luke 16:1-9 we find Jesus teaching His disciples the Parable of the Unjust Steward, as it is traditionally called. Look with me at the NIV translation of the passage:

> Jesus told His disciples: "There was a rich man whose manager was accused of wasting his possessions. So he called him in and asked him, 'What is this I hear about you? Give an account of your management, because you cannot be manager any longer.'
>
> "The manager said to himself, 'What shall I do now? My master is taking away my job. I'm not strong enough to dig, and I'm ashamed to beg—I know what I'll do so that, when I lose my job here, people will welcome me into their houses.'
>
> "So he called in each one of his master's debtors. He asked the first, 'How much do you owe my master?'
>
> " 'Eight hundred gallons of olive oil,' he replied.
>
> "The manager told him, 'Take your bill, sit down quickly, and make it four hundred.'
>
> "Then he asked the second, 'And how much do you owe?'
>
> " 'A thousand bushels of wheat,' he replied.
>
> "He told him, 'Take your bill and make it eight hundred.'
>
> "The master commended the dishonest manager because he had acted shrewdly. For the people of this world are more shrewd in dealing with their own kind than are the people of the light."

That is the parable, and if you stop to think about it, when coupled with Jesus telling it, it becomes a very hilarious story. Either the rich boss was touched with the heat, or dead drunk, or he knew something we don't know. For example, he may have known that his debtors were bad risks and that he was lucky to get anything out of them at all. Or perhaps the regional economy was mired in such huge debt that no one in Palestine was paying his bills—thus getting part of what was owed seemed better than getting nothing at all. But Jesus presented none of these conditions as part of the story. It must be therefore that Jesus had a most unusual point to make. He had, in the language of our day, a card up his sleeve.

The ridiculously unexpected approval given to the transactions by the rich man who was taking a big loss is what makes the story funny. Groucho Marx could have played the rich man's role perfectly with a straight face and a cigar; people would have laughed heartily. (He once acted as a hotel lobby clerk who tore up all the letters in the guests' mailboxes. They laughed at that, too.)

Jesus did draw a conclusion. He pointed out that the manager was shrewder than the "sons of light" because he had made himself someone worth cultivating with a view to friendship. I am not personally making any effort to explain this parable, or to justify the manager's ploy, or to pass judgment on what might seem to be Jesus' approval of a dishonest transaction. I'm only saying that if you take away the humor, this parable turns back into the insoluble problem it has been to doctors of the church over the centuries.

Professor James S. Stewart (my teacher at Edinburgh University) interpreted the rich man's commendation of his manager lightly. He has the boss saying, "My word, you *are* an astute and daring rascal! For barefaced coolness, you have got us all beaten hollow!"—which makes the response sound all the more funny and peculiar. But Professor Stewart goes on to explain that the rich man "is not God, he is any man of the world—nothing else." He then makes this powerful point: "What Christ is fixing on is the one salient truth He is after: God's people might well take an occasional lesson from God's enemies—the saint has something to learn from the sinner."[2] It seems the children of this world are sometimes wiser—more resourceful and far-seeing, more inventive and purposeful when caught in a jam—than are we "children of light" when we confront a genuine crisis.

My own conclusion is that this story adds to the evidence that Jesus had a highly-developed sense of humor, and I believe that He inherited it from His smiling heavenly Father. As Jesus addressed the people of His day who were being overwhelmed by their problems, He said to them in effect, "Look at this man. He didn't keep on whining about his plight. He used his ingenuity to make a couple of clever bargains. They were so clever that even his master commended him." Now, that is broad humor. It's crazy. The man cheated, but nobody is accusing him. He broke the law, but so what? If the parable proves anything, it is that in real life strange things happen. God may offer more than one way to cut a deal, or make a point, or settle a debt, or raise the joy level.

It may trouble some Christians to imagine Jesus as laughing, when He is supposed to be the Man of Sorrows, but the truth is that laughter never was banned from the early Christian church, and shouldn't be banned now. As an old Shaker philosopher, Brother Calvin Fairchild, once said, "Good, round, hearty, side-shaking laughter is healthy for everybody." The *Encyclopedia Britannica* observes that laughter "beguiles the present"—that is, laughter charms and diverts the present just as hope helps us to face the future. It is a gift from God, and we ought to hang onto it and thank Him every day for it.

GOD SMILES AND INTERVENES

Since this chapter deals with the Joy of the Lord as it expresses itself in amusement, it might help to describe my own exposure to divine comedy.

After yielding to my own brothers' persuasion and deciding to enter the ministry (without ever actually receiving a call from God), I looked for encouragement and support wherever I could find it. I informed my former college fraternity president of my decision. This friend, a tall, distinguished-looking young man, had already made a name for himself in the wine industry. I had always looked up to him. So I telephoned him, revealed my plan, and waited for his reaction. A pregnant silence was followed by his answer in a deep voice: "Frankly, Sherwood, I can't fancy you in the pulpit!"

Call it an honest reaction. Call it what you wish; I took it as a heavy blow. This was to be my life! Of course I could say by way of excuse that this fraternity brother did not attend church, that he knew nothing of theological education, and so on; but there it was. He had known me for several years, and gave as he thought a correct opinion. Because he did not really miss the mark, I squirmed.

Years later, even after I had graduated from seminary *cum laude*, had studied theologians from Karl Barth to Carl Henry, had obtained my Ph.D. in Scotland, and had sat under some of the great preachers of the day, I still kept hearing those words rolling around in the back of my cranium: "I can't fancy you in the pulpit."

At first I simply brushed them off, thinking that everybody has detractors. When they failed to disappear, I decided the statement was creating a psychological block for me; that I was letting those words become pestiferous through repetition. I even wondered if the devil was using them to discourage me and keep me silent. The truth was I had been a country mile from the Lord for years, and in all honesty my pulpit presence was not exactly setting the world on fire.

One day, after reading my Bible, I reflected on how bluntly the Lord reacted to some of the more obstinate characters in the Old Testament. He wasted no words, especially when He dealt with their pride and their failure to acknowledge His presence in their actions. Sitting in my study, I heard those ugly words again: "I can't fancy you in the pulpit." But this time I seemed to hear *THE LORD* saying the words and adding something more: **"In My house, I don't fancy ANYONE ELSE in My pulpit. WHOSE PULPIT DO YOU THINK IT IS?"**

Well, I was so astonished I started to laugh. Of course! How stupid of me. By myself I was no better in the pulpit than an orangutan. By myself I was simply babbling other people's words, a windy clergyman making noises that so wearied the congregation that it almost felt like singing, "If I had wings like an angel / Over these prison walls I would fly."

In God's pulpit I had been no more than a mouse that squeaked. Now God had picked up my fraternity brother's words and had used them to show me that even though His truth is sometimes conveyed in odd packages, if it actually comes from the portals of heaven, it carries its own validity.

So now the Lord had my attention. Barth had something right—God was indeed "totally Other." I was learning that beyond preachers and sermons and homiletics and church buildings and janitors, the pulpit itself was *His own* private sacred desk, the King of Heaven's royal pulpit, to be used for the proclamation of His holy Word. The human voices He made use of to communicate were just that—voices; their significance lay not in the attractiveness of the messengers, but in the faithfulness of the message of Jesus Christ that the human voices were summoned to proclaim.

I could be a bellhop, I could be a lobster fisherman, I could be a donkey like Balaam's ass. Or I could be myself. God didn't "fancy" me or anybody else in His pulpit, but He might use me if I shut my driveling mouth, ceased all pretensions, and let Him speak.

As I continued to chuckle at my brashness, the question came to me, Really, what was I trying to prove? And that question reminded me of the counsel I once received from a wise Scottish lady, Miss Margaret Romanes: "*A saint is a person who knows how to get out of God's way.*"

It took a very long time for the grace of God to work in me—and even longer for me to discover how much fun God was having with me. Even now in retirement, when an occasional invitation to preach comes my way, I find myself chuckling at the humor of God. At age 88 I was invited to address some high schoolers at a Christian camp. As I accepted, God's funny message seemed to come right back: "I can't fancy you, but be My guest."

I spoke for an hour, and after I had finished, 350 high schoolers rose and thanked me—but Someone else had been in charge. They were applauding the wrong person. The Holy Spirit had been at work, joy was flowing, and God was smiling on me again. Some fun. He was again reminding me that He is God, the Ruler of the universe, and that the gospel pulpit forever belongs to Him and to no one else. As for my rather uneven contribution—just who did I fancy I was?

DELIGHTED IN HIS PRESENCE

A profitable way to start looking for the Joy of the Lord is to remember that while God is indeed running the whole creation, He has a subtle sense of humor. In fact, Rees Howells, the great Welsh prayer warrior, used to say, "The Holy Spirit is full of jokes."[3]

It's difficult to communicate such an idea in today's market. The media are professionally interested in the grisly things that happen to human beings far more than they are in the joyful things. Telephone, e-mail, postal service, fax, radio, and television all flood us with solemn warnings and dire threats of imminent dangers from fifty thousand sources. Books and magazines alarm us with dark, menacing problems I never heard of or knew existed. The result is an unending, reverberating thundercloud of angst and dread (not to mention heartburn) that is rolling over the world in this third millennium after Jesus' birth.

How does one come up for air? How does one bubble up to the surface of this murky flood into which we have been dunked? How do you and I summon the chariot of heavenly joy to "swing low" for us? We're not really demanding ebullience, trembling excitement, or swooning ecstasy. We just want to live in the Spirit and have a little fun: chocolate-chip cookies, double rainbows, a Bach chorale, a hole in one, a child talking to Jesus, people of different backgrounds enjoying each other, a buddy asking for prayer and getting it, a church on fire with love, a well-cooked, relaxing dinner, a pleasantly-written book with a gratifying ending, some favorite music, a banana cream pie...

Because I am editor emeritus of *Decision* Magazine, each year there comes to our home a different, well-executed calendar painting featuring a Royal Canadian Mounted Policeman, courtesy of the Potlatch Paper Company of Minnesota. Every one of these painted scenes is brilliantly fresh, but a recent one proved unusually interesting to me. In it the artist, A. Friberg, featured a tall Mountie in full uniform, with broadbrimmed hat, scarlet jacket, striped dark trousers, and highpolish boots. He is listening to a small boy and his older sister. Beneath his broad hat the officer's head is tilted toward them.

In the background is a log home nestled among pine and fir trees, and there are mountains. The RCMP steed is alongside, a pet terrier is keeping watch, and each child is holding a tiny kitten. As the children look up at the quiet expression on the officer's face, the boy is obviously saying something to the man, and the man is listening. At the same time the little girl's face is uplifted, laughing and radiant. To her the Mountie's visit is obviously a delight, and her laughter reveals the depth of her joy.

Here is the voice of impressive authority standing before them, and yet the two children have absolutely no fear. There is no evil presence, no complaining, no worrisome problem in the scene, just sheer delight. The children are at ease. Warmth and beauty and utter confidence are present. This scene becomes to me a metaphor of our relationship as believers to God the Father Almighty. We are His children. We are fully aware of His majesty, His authority, and His unlimited power; yet we come unafraid into His presence and smile, even laugh, as we talk with Him. To bask in His love is to know true peace. To feel His presence, to walk in His ways, is to know the freedom we have in Christ and the genuine Joy of the Lord.

Is the Mounted Policeman smiling in the painting? No, he is not. He is on patrol. But even on duty he welcomes the smiles and is responsive to what the young Canadians are asking. He shows it.

God our Father is not on patrol; and as for duty, He created it. He *is* Duty, but He never lets duty supersede or lessen His love for us. In the heavenly scheme duty, like everything else, is subordinated to love. God loves us. That is why He is the God who smiles; that is why His smile can lead to our joyful laughter. Even today He is smiling on us, although many, many people in our environment find it hard to believe. That is the message of the Book of Books, and it is still true in the third millennium.

13
DOES GOD'S SMILE REALLY MATTER TO US?

❧

"So how do I get this elusive Joy of the Lord that comes from the smile of God? What do I have to do?"

People keep asking, and we will try again. God's joy is not on the open market. It is therefore not obtainable "for a consideration." On the other hand we can have it without even lifting a finger or holding out a hand, because it is already with us and within us. How much does an attitude weigh? How much muscular effort does it take to smile?

In Psalm 40:8 we read this expression: "I delight to do Your will, O my God." Point of order—What is God's will? Jesus said God wants us to spread the gospel of love, to carry it into all the world. All right, let's suppose we try to do that quite apart from joy. We will take no spiritual joy in sharing the gospel, and no delight in helping people to come out of sin's broom closet and start to breathe the fresh air of salvation in Christ. How will that work?

We can find out quickly by looking at the efforts of two Bible teachers in Scripture, one a prophet and the other an apostle. These two individuals were both Hebrews. Jonah was a prophet in the Old Testament. Paul wrote nearly two-fifths of the New Testament. Both men were brought up in the fear of God, and both were commissioned by God to execute His wishes. Each fulfilled his assignment with distinction. And there the similarities end.

The book of Jonah tells us that prophet did not like his orders.[1] God told him to warn the people of Nineveh of His coming judgment and to call them to repent of their sins. He rejected the order, tried to evade it, but God eventually forced him against his will to discharge his duty.

The book of Acts tells us that Paul, a brand-new convert, was called by God to carry the good news of Jesus Christ to "Gentiles" and "Kings" as well as to the people of Israel.[2] Linguistically prepared in both the Greek and Aramaic languages as well as in Hebrew, he accepted the commission with joy.

Jonah tried to evade his orders by skipping town. He embarked on a ship bound for Tarshish as a paid passenger. But when a storm arose at sea, the crew pinned the blame on Jonah—correctly. At his own suggestion, they threw him overboard and the storm subsided. A very large specimen of Mediterranean sea life then delivered the prophet to a Palestinian beach. In due course he received the same orders a second time.

Paul the apostle proceeded to spread the gospel of Jesus Christ on two continents with remarkable success. He did it by working with teams of men and women of many different languages and backgrounds. He established the church of Jesus Christ in cities where every other religion had failed to attract, and where it is alive and flourishing today. Paul may not have drawn the crowds that Jonah did in Nineveh, but the adventure of his travel itinerary has never been matched, his ministry has flourished, and for 2000 years his name has been honored and his gospel accepted with joy by millions of readers of the New Testament.

Jonah did effective work in Nineveh, the Assyrian capital, with amazing spiritual results, but he labored alone and definitely did not enjoy either his work or its results, since Israel considered Assyria its mortal enemy. When God found that the people of Nineveh were repenting as a result of Jonah's preaching, He lifted His judgment and spared the city. This so angered Jonah that he wished he were dead.[3]

PREACHING GOD'S SMILE

So here were these two men, both sent by God, both working with people of different nationalities and tongues, both achieving positive results. What made the difference?

Jonah considered the assignment a burden. He tried hard to get out of it, and when he did preach in Nineveh, he disliked the bountiful results of God's smile upon the Ninevites. Because he wanted that smile for no other people than his own, he was not able to share in God's joy over the city's repentance.

Paul found the work in Asia exciting. He loved it, and he loved the people. He was convinced that God's smile mattered to him and to everyone he met. The book of Acts records that when Paul and his companion Barnabas were leaving Antioch in Pisidia, they left behind as the fruit of their ministry new disciples, new converts, new Jewish and Gentile Christians. And how did the team feel about their work? "The disciples were filled with joy and with the Holy Spirit."[4]

When the two missionaries reached Lystra, an uproarious scene developed after God used Paul to heal a man with crippled feet. Lystra being an Asian city traditionally devoted to the pagan Greek gods, the people looked upon Barnabas as Zeus in human form, and they supposed Paul to be Hermes, the messenger of the gods. The temple priest ordered bulls and garlands brought to the city gates and encouraged the crowd to offer sacrifices to the men. Barnabas and Paul were hard put to prove their humanity, but in doing so, they preached the good news of the kingdom and told the Lycaonians that God not only provided them with seasonal rains and food, but He also "fills your hearts with joy."[5]

Later, when Paul and Silas sailed across to Macedonia to plant the gospel in Europe, they ran into fresh opposition and suddenly found themselves in a jail in Philippi, after having been soundly whipped. At midnight they were still wide awake and no doubt in pain, but were overflowing with joy by the Holy Spirit. They filled the dark, dank prison with psalms and hymns and spiritual songs that amazed and entertained the other prisoners.[6] What ebullience! What dauntless spirits! These two men exhibited an invincible quality of life that has always been characteristic of Christianity at its best—a quality which most certainly radiates the attitude of our Lord Jesus Christ Himself.

Some scholars still claim that Paul had no sense of humor, but it seems to me that is exactly what he did have, spilling over. Tell me, what kind of man would put his life at deadly risk again and again in hostile foreign countries if he didn't have to? The only answer I know is, either he is a complete idiot, or else a Christian missionary who is committed to his Lord, who knows that the smile of God matters to the human race, and who is filled with the same lightness of heart and overflowing joy that spills across so many pages of the New Testament.

Think again of Paul and Silas in that Philippian jail, singing praises in the darkness. When an earthquake shook the jail into rubble and the frightened jailer wanted to kill himself, Paul and Silas told him to stop, that nobody in his prison wanted to escape. Their conduct so impressed the jailer that he asked them how he could be saved. They told him. He was convinced, converted, and baptized, and before the night ended the jailer had fed Paul and Silas and had attended to the same wounds that he, possibly, had ordered inflicted. And how did the jailer feel about his demolished calaboose? We don't know. How did his family feel about the earthquake? We don't know that either. All we are told is that God filled the whole family with joy because they had come to believe in Him.[7]

If that were not enough, when morning came and the city magistrate ordered Paul and Silas released, they refused to go without an official escort. They announced that they were Roman citizens, which exempted them from brutality and harassment from the local constabulary. A beautiful touch! The bureaucracy panicked and dispatched an official escort to the jail. As Halford Luccock expressed it, "With sore backs and heads held high" (and no doubt with smiles on their faces) the two ambassadors of the Lord strode out through the broken prison gates of Philippi and into the chronicles of sacred history.[8] God, too, was smiling.

Nearly everywhere Paul took the gospel, whether to Pisidian Antioch, Iconium, Lystra, Thessalonica, Derbe, Corinth, Berea, Ephesus, or Jerusalem, uproar resulted. Yet the man himself seemed to be in the eye of the hurricane, untroubled in spirit. "Keep up your courage," he told the half-drowned sailors aboard the foundering ship that held him prisoner. "Get something to eat. You're going to survive, all of you."[9]

On the island of Malta after the shipwreck, when a poisonous snake bit him on the hand, Paul casually shook it off into the fire. When he reached Italy, a delegation of Christians met him. They had traveled 43 miles from Rome to greet him at the marketplace of Appius.[10] In response, Paul gave thanks to God for them and told them to take courage.

In a letter to the Christians of Corinth, Paul expressed his feelings and those of his companions vividly:

> We are hard pressed on every side, but not crushed; perplexed, but not in despair; persecuted, but not abandoned; struck down, but not destroyed. We always carry around in our body the death of Jesus, so that the life of Jesus may also be revealed in our body....[We are] sorrowful, yet always rejoicing....In all our troubles my joy knows no bounds.[11]

Joy! It is the one key word that distinguishes the authentic Paul from all the spurious and imitative letters attributed to him in the early centuries of the Christian era. Paul wrote again and again of his inner joy; his imitators did not.

How then do we "get" the Joy of the Lord? How do we come to bask in God's smile? We have seen that Paul the apostle had that joy; Jonah the prophet did not. Paul was convinced that God's smile of love upon all mankind mattered; Jonah kept that smile to himself. So we see that Paul did not "get" the joy—he took it with him, and gave away his joy and the warmth of God's smile everywhere he went. This made his ministry doubly effective. He both glorified God and enjoyed Him. A Jew from a foreign land (Israel), a one-time persecutor and no doubt killer of Christians, Paul won his way into the hearts of people all over Asia Minor and Greece with his cheerful, friendly approach and his indomitable Spirit of love in Christ.

When people embrace Jesus Christ, something mysterious rubs off. What is it? Can you define it? Can you examine it under a microscope? It's not just a metaphor or some other figure of speech, because it is real. It seems to be something that goes along with these people, and yet they may not be aware of it. Dogmatically it could be called the sanctifying grace of God. Emotionally it is a sweet memory of close contact with the Savior. Volitionally it is a powerful force, for it sets the human will on fire. Scientifically it cannot be seen under the microscope, but *it is there and it is real.*

This mysterious rub-off is the Joy of the Lord, a gift of the Holy Spirit. It is a glorious, unbounded pleasure and gladness that comes straight from the smiling God Himself. When we share the love of Jesus with others, we give it away, and it comes back to us in full measure. Then we have it, cake and frosting too. Hallelujah!

OUR HEARTS FIND GLADNESS IN HIM

14
THE JOY FACTOR

≈

A man's wisdom makes his face shine,
And the sternness of his face is changed.

—ECCLESIASTES 8:1

At the beginning of this book I mentioned that a television producer asked me some thoughtful questions on the subject of joy during an interview on a Christian channel in Chicago. I'm afraid my replies at that time were rather impromptu. I kept the questions, and now perhaps I can better respond. Each question was specifically designed to challenge the idea of a God who smiles and to investigate a gospel that actually promises to bring joy into our lives. We shall take them in order:

"You speak of God having a smile on His face. We don't often think of God that way, do we?"

"No, we don't think that way because, as Dr. Freud said, people like to create a deity in their own image, and in our own image many of us are not smiling either. But the God we Christians love and worship is not a blown-up *homo sapiens*. He is the living Lord, the King of creation, and the heavenly Father of all who love and worship Him. It's not hard for me to picture such a wonderful God as smiling."

"You say that the Bible itself places a high priority on joy. How so?"

"I would single out particularly the book of Isaiah, the Psalms, and certain passages in the New Testament. The truth is, however, that expressions of joy and gladness are scattered through the entire Scriptures. I would also point to the joy-filled festivals of the Jewish people in the Old Testament, which speak for themselves."

"How did the joy that Jesus had, and that He conveyed to others, affect the New Testament church?"

"It bowled the disciples over. They had never seen anything like it. That's why they left their fishing nets and went with Jesus. Of course it was not all joy. Much of the gospel narrative as it stands is taken up with conflict, and rightly so, for our Lord had a mission to carry out, and it drew opposition from the start. But apart from all the controversies we can find clear suggestions that the sunny effect Jesus' person had on the people as a whole, disciples included, seems to have been nothing short of sensational.

"To take one illustration: At Pentecost the joy of the disciples appeared so evident that bystanders made fun of them, thinking they were drunk. Peter refuted the charge and then preached a sermon in which he quoted from Psalm 16: 'My heart is glad and my tongue rejoices... You will fill me with joy in your presence.'[1] When he finished, 3000 people were baptized into the Christian faith. As time went on, 'The Lord added to their number daily those who were being saved.'[2]

"From the record, it would appear the early church was clearly a joy-filled congregation."

"Do Christians really understand what the Joy of the Lord is all about?"

"Nobody really understands the ways of God. Paul admitted, 'Who has known the mind of the LORD? Or who has become His counselor?'[3] When we use the expression 'the Joy of our Lord,' I suggest that we think of it as an attribute of the Triune God, but not exclusively so. Jesus also taught us to think of His joy as a state of mind and heart that He imparts *to us,* just as He imparted it to His disciples after His resurrection: 'The disciples were overjoyed when they saw the Lord.' "[4]

"Is joy then a blessing, something we today can actually receive into our own hearts?"

"Definitely. And I would add 'with music!' Jesus ended his greatest parable (Luke 15) with a burst of music. When John saw the Lamb standing on Mount Zion (Revelation 14), he heard the sound of harps. I have noticed that musically inclined Christians appear to recognize easily the Joy of the Lord and to feel at home in it. Look for them together: God, music, and joy.

"I remember years ago taking a step toward believing in Jesus just by joining a joyful group singing around a piano. The song?

O the depth of the riches, the riches of love,
The riches of love in Christ Jesus.
Far better than gold or wealth untold
Are the riches of love in Christ Jesus."[5]

"Do we Christians experience much joy in our lives?"

"Yes. Terrific joy! Time after time. It depends of course on how well Christ is 'formed in us' spiritually,[6] and how deeply Jesus comes into our lives, and how much His love affects us. The Holy Spirit can and will bring joy, as the gospel teaches us, even during hours of dire tribulation. My friend Robert Munger says it well: 'The New Testament will do what it says it will do.' "

"What is the biggest barrier to joy?"

"I would say it is my own self, M-Y-S-E-L-F. When I set my own agenda, everything else is secondary, including joy. Let me quote from Ulrich Zwingli, the brilliant sixteenth-century

Swiss Reformer: 'Man increasingly loves himself, seeks to please himself, trusts himself, credits everything to himself, thinks that he sees what is straight and what is crooked, and believes that what he approves everyone ought to approve, even his Creator.'[7] Make no mistake, that is a barrier. It has to come down. It requires unconditional surrender, and once that takes place, joy is often the first thing to break in through the broken barrier."

"How can we have joy despite difficult circumstances?"

"The apostle Paul wrote to the Corinthians, 'In all things we commend ourselves as ministers of God: in much patience, in tribulations, in needs, in distresses...as sorrowful, yet always rejoicing...as having nothing, and yet possessing all things.'[8] It was for the 'joy set before Him' that our Savior Jesus Christ endured the cross'.[9] It is the great Christian secret: a loving joy that overcomes the world and its punishments and predicaments. It is a gift of the Holy Spirit, and what is more, it can be ours."

"Many people in America feel as though there is nothing to be joyful about. What would you say to these people?"

"I would start with the miracle of our breathing. To inhabit a living body calls for considerable gratefulness and joy. We can thank God for the pumping heart, the circulating blood, the eyes, the ears, the limbs, the fingers. I heard of an old lady who had only two teeth left, but who thanked the Lord every day because they 'hit.'

"At our house there is joy every week when the trash truck comes around, not to speak of the mail truck. When the water system breaks down, there is joy when the plumber arrives. When a neighbor says 'good morning,' and you think of what he could have said, and might well have said, how can you say that there is nothing in America to be joyful about?

"We can find joy in our children and grandchildren, and in just having friends, the kind of friends who share blessings with us and want to join us in thanking God for those same blessings. Then loving pets can bring us yet a different kind of joy. Further, we should never take for granted the gift of living in a free land for which we can be joyfully grateful.

"Above all, the Bible is an ever-flowing fountain of joy, assuming we know where to look. Make it Number One on your reading list. I once heard Evangelist Mordecai Ham, who preached the sermon that brought Billy Graham to the altar, say with a frowning expression, 'I pick up my paper to see what man has been doing.' He added with a smile, 'Then I pick up my Bible to see what God is going to do.'

"In addition to the Bible, Christian books and films can become highly encouraging sources of joy. But everything will come together in our joyful prayer of thanksgiving to God for His goodness in loving us and saving our souls forever in Christ Jesus."

"What role does prayer play in our having joy?"

"Prayer plays an opening role, particularly the prayer of praise that exalts God and thanks Him for blessings already 'present and accounted for.' The Holy Spirit will use that prayer to start the juices flowing and the smiles smiling. We begin to feel better, not just because of what we have, but because of the goodness of God who gave it to us. There is even joy in the prayer of anticipation that is based on God's loving-kindness and our own hopes."

"What are some examples of Christians whose joy is evident in their lives?"

"Anyone can compile a list of such examples in history, such as Francis of Assisi, Lady Julian of Norwich, Brother Lawrence of the Resurrection, Billy Bray, Corrie ten Boom,

Mother Teresa, and others lesser known. I could include my own mother, Harriet Eliot Benton Wirt, who taught me to pray and who had a lovely laugh. But I prefer to let the reader compile his or her own list of exemplary joyful Christians—and long may it grow!

"I disqualify myself from this list. Like Augustine, I came late to the Lord, and when I did come it was not in search of love or joy so much as spiritual strength. I felt my sermons were weak; and as for the listeners in the pews, they were already behaving better than I! One day in 1954 I finally sat in a 'victory circle,' took the Bible as God's Word, and declared to God and myself that from that day I was an evangelical believer. There was no response among the angels in heaven; or if there was, I was not informed. Nor did anybody at the time explain to me what Ken Blue says in one of his books, namely, that 'to come to God is to come to joy.' "[10]

"How important is the joy factor in Christian living?"

"It is not for me to say. How important is a smile in the morning? A bouquet at a wedding? A cold glass of water, given in love on a hot day? The psalmist wrote long ago, 'I will go to the altar of God, to God my exceeding joy; and on the harp I will praise You.'[11] How important was the harp?

"Jesus taught His disciples to pray and then added, 'Until now you have not asked for anything in my name. Ask and you will receive, and your joy will be complete.'[12] He doesn't even mention some really important things in our lives—things like our reputations, our long-range ethical goals, our desires to be good citizens and friendly neighbors, even our longing for holiness. Instead he talks about completing our joy! Well, it's about time we realized how importantly the Bible treats it. As Ken Blue rightly says, 'Joy is at the heart of the Christian experience.'[13]

"If revival comes to the church of God in this new century (and I pray it will), I doubt that it will come with the trappings of power—political, scientific, or religious. But it will certainly come with joy. When it comes, the media may have trouble discerning it and even more reporting it. Marketing experts may search their laptops in vain to locate it. Imagine revival on the Internet! Lord, come quickly!

"Knowing God's sense of humor and His wonderful smile, I half-suspect that His Spirit will bring revival through some highly unlikely people in some unlikely place. The cues for Christians will be the biblical signs of authenticity, such as the cross, repentance, restitution, and love. When it comes, may it turn us all anew to the freshness of the gospel, the outpouring of the Holy Spirit, and the overwhelming joy of the risen Jesus. Hallelujah!"

15
THE JOY OF OBEDIENCE

∾

Trust and obey, for there's no other way
To be happy in Jesus, but to trust and obey.

he word "obedience" has stuck in the craw of the human race for so many centuries that I have decided to begin this chapter, as I did the first chapter, by asking myself some straight questions:

"Why should I obey anybody?"

"You won't last long if you don't."

"Whom should I obey?"

"God, first of all. "

"My first ancestor didn't obey Him."

"Yes, and look at the trouble he started."

"You mean, she started."

"Don't quibble. Obey God, and you shall live."

"You mean, obey the Ten Commandments, or obey Christ? Which?"

"Both."

"I see. Well, I'm a free person. Where's the payoff in all this obedience? Where's the fun?"

"Obey. You will find out."

"One other point. Does your God ever stop smiling?"

"You will find that out, too."

OUR DIFFICULTY WITH OBEDIENCE

When the word "obedience" is mentioned today in Western society, it is often given a cool reception. In fact, obedience was the one word of the English language I disliked as a little boy. "Why should I obey? What is the point? Why can't I do what I feel like doing, instead of what someone else wants?" This got me into trouble.

During the '20s, I learned to recognize authority as a Boy Scout. Those were postwar days of intense patriotism. I loved to read about Bunker Hill and Nathan Hale and Washington crossing the Delaware. As a sophomore ROTC corporal at a land-grant university, I marched on parade in uniform twice a week, proud to be an American.

Then came Hitler, and Churchill, and war in Europe. I remember 1940 as a year when intense antiwar feeling swept across our nation. Respect for government decreased. Opposition spread against any participation in combat, and it grew until a different enemy made a direct attack on our soil at Pearl Harbor and the Aleutian islands.

By the time the American people had suffered through the horrendous losses of life in World War II, the Korean "United Nations Action," and the Vietnam debacle, words like patriotism, loyalty, obedience, and authority had inevitably lost their appeal to much of our rank and file. But even more significant and much more tragic, the basic moral ideals of Western civilization had also been brought into widespread contempt.

None of this became fully apparent to me until an incident occurred at my own school, the University of California at Berkeley, in the year 1964. A campus policeman made a routine arrest, as I recall, and a crowd of students then surrounded his car and kept the officer captive inside for two days and nights. No effort was ever made to relieve the officer, either by government agencies or the university administration.

This signal expression of public disobedience in American life came to me and to others as a shock, for it developed into full-fledged student unrest that spread across the country. I no longer blame the students alone, for experience has since taught me that the degeneration of Western society, both public and private, has been going on ever since those terrible days in World War I when the lingering vestiges of Victorian social conduct were drowned in the blood-soaked trenches of Belgium and France.

Now for my conclusion: The chief obstacle to America's survival as a nation is not our failure to deal successfully with such social problems as drugs, guns, traffic, divorce, porn, or high-tech corruption. The present unhappiness (I don't call it a malaise) in America can be laid to the fact that we, for the most part, have either forgotten or never learned how to obey.

Concurrent with and resulting from this lack of obedience is the spread of a disenchanted, rebellious spirit that is evident in nearly every agency of North American life: education, security, business, finance, politics, family life, communication, transportation, athletics, and religion. It shows itself in every form of government, including the legislative, executive, and judicial.

Don't categorize me as a doomsayer or a hopeless cynic. This negative spirit is not to be confused with sickness, let alone with original sin. Sickness cannot be cured by an act of the will. Original sin cannot be removed by a decision. Our problem is simply that we have forgotten how to take orders and have therefore refused to obey. Our discipline is gone with the wind. But we may yet be enabled to remember and do what is needed. God is still smiling, life is still a beautiful miracle, and His divine grace is as powerful as ever.

We Americans all need to reassure ourselves that ours is a noble commonwealth, blessed of God and endowed with a magnificent heritage. America still has a good Constitution and is not falling apart. Our citizens as a whole want to be good people and to enjoy a good life. Unfortunately we are part of a generation that has had great difficulty in learning obedience either to God or man.

OBEDIENCE AND FREEDOM

If it is true that the student rioters of the '60s had no basic plan whatever except to disobey, today we are reaping that harvest. In fact, in the twenty-first century I see only one remaining strong American force that seriously attempts to maintain the rule of law. Such a force is unique in a land filled with millions of competing, lawbreaking individualists who prefer to obey absolutely no one.

I may have trouble identifying this force in a way that will convince readers in the twenty-first century. It is not the federal government. It is not the police. It is not the church—I wish it were. Instead, I see it as the military. I'm sure that will rouse a sharp protest, for many people today seem convinced that the armed forces of the United States, like every other social entity, no longer follow the moral principles of our founding fathers. Military obedience today is considered by many to be simply a pragmatic means of operation rather than a noble response to a great cause like human freedom.

As a veteran of World War II, I don't feel that way. I always loved the American flag and what it stood for, and I loved those who defended it. When I graduated from my university in 1932, heavily in debt, it took years of struggle during the Great Depression before I was free of it. Then while some American youths went through an undisciplined childhood and emerged into a wayward adolescence and cynical maturity, I and some others put on our uniforms and learned how to take and carry out orders.

I realize now that our history professors, while giving us background on democracy and politics, failed to tell us that America was actually put together on discipline and the obeying of orders. We were assured that we had inherited a singularly great country, but we were never told how we got it—how we won our freedom in the Revolutionary War. It was not because of our superior statesmanship in devising a republic with divisions of power and two-party systems. It was not because of the Federalist Papers or the presence of the French fleet.

We won our country because thousands of young Americans decided to fight for it. They left home and placed themselves in complete obedience to one man, General George Washington. This man told them what to do, when to do it, and when to stop, and they obeyed him. They even died for him. That is what won our freedom: obedience to the death. The young colonists gave up their families and personal liberties to take on the yoke of obedience so that a new, free nation would be born under God. Who today remembers that it was the response of the colonial troops at Valley Forge and elsewhere to the commands of General Washington and his officers, and *only that obedience,* that made our golden political future a reality?

Today we Americans still wax loud in extolling and cherishing our political independence. "Live free or die" is carried on one state's license plate. But as General Eisenhower wrote, "Freedom from fear and injustice and oppression will be ours only in the measure that men who value such freedom are ready to defend it."

Right now the publishing houses are bursting with books about leadership. I never was a leader, never wanted to be—but I wanted leaders I could obey. Today I don't see much help coming from billionaire Doonesburys with their latest computers and diagrams and projections on the Internet. I see true leadership as emerging from disciplined, capable, informed young Americans of principle who love their country and have learned how to take orders and carry them out. Not, let me add, how to cut a crooked deal, or work an angle, or pull off a coup, or steal an election.

America today needs God-fearing men and women of skill, perception, balance, and achievement, who have come up through the ranks and earned their way by obeying orders. They will be honored by their country not with plaques and titles and high positions and useless medals, not to speak of bird-spattered statues—they will be honored with leadership.

THE JOY OF DOING RIGHT

That leads me to a higher question than civil obedience. What about God Himself? The Bible calls on men and women to give absolute obedience to the one true God.[1] As we enter the new millennium, it is not always clear just what that entails. In Old Testament times the clerical emphasis was on obedience to God's law, which included all His statutes, testimonies, judgments, commandments, strictures, and precepts: "Do this, and you will live."[2]

In the New Testament the call to obedience shifted, as believers in Jesus Christ were justified before God by faith, as Paul says, and not by the works of the law, "for by the works of the law no flesh shall be justified."[3] Instead, the early Christians were called to rely on the Person and teachings of the Lord Jesus Christ, and the writings of His apostles.

I find in the centuries following that scholars, theologians, preachers, and monks were spending too little time on the joys of obedience and rather too much on the sins of disobedience. We were warned, we were chided, we were threatened with all kinds of severe penalties for our lawbreaking and wrongdoing. But as I now understand the original text, the real purpose of obedience to the Triune God was not the avoidance of wrong, but the thrill and glory and joy of doing right!

I don't care a fig tree's fig for all the ghastly punishments for disobedience that spewed from the mouths of the ancients, because they don't touch me. When I became a Christian, my heart and soul were sealed by the Holy Spirit. I gave my life to Jesus Christ, not out of obedience but in obedience and out of sheer love. That life (what is left of it) now belongs to Him, and Him I obey.

I would go further and declare that for persons seeking God, the gospel challenge of obedience to God has been befogged by all the continued threats and warnings of severe punishment for disobedience. That emphasis is as far from the true message of the Lord Jesus as night is from day. Jesus, you remember, told us, "My yoke is easy and My burden is light."[4] Not that the punitive element is a mistaken idea; on the contrary, it is very real. But it is *not* the reason why we ought to obey God.

Let's suppose we are living in one of the American states and someone—anyone—in civil authority over us issues an order. We are given two choices: We can obey the order or disobey it. Its stated purpose is to accomplish something positive to promote the general welfare. For us to carry out the order would be, generally speaking, helpful in making things better.

Now suppose our own decision to obey the order has nothing to do with the purpose. We obey simply because we are told to do it, and because if we don't do it we will be fined, jailed, put in stocks, or punished in whatever way is popular at the moment. The *threat* behind the order is what makes us do what we're told.

I say that is a rancid state of affairs. It violates the social contract of a nation, and it lacks the touch of Jesus. We should be glad to obey the order simply because it is the right thing to do and because it accomplishes something for the common good. Who cares about threats and penalties? But that is why, in our so-called enlightened age, so many citizens find the idea of obedience unattractive.

Now, when it comes to obeying Almighty God (who requires absolute obedience) many Christian people frankly see it as a duty and obligation. They say something like this: "God orders me to worship Him, so I'll go to church." So off we go 1) just because He told us to; or 2) because someone insisted it was our duty to go; or 3) because our own conscience pricks us into going. All of those reasons miss the point. Who do you think God is? He is not a stern schoolmaster with a whip. He loves you. Duty is not and never can be the immortal good news of the gospel of Jesus. God wants us in His house because He loves us, and He wants to give us joy!

OBEDIENCE GIVES US A GLIMPSE OF HEAVEN

To worship God is in itself a glorious treat. We sense His smiling presence, we feel His love, we move into the exalted realm of the Spirit, and for a little while we are in loving communion with heaven. Jesus seems to come anew and dwell in our hearts. By faith we become lyrical. We sing, we kneel, we lift our hands, we smile, and there is joy in our hearts. We realize that we are sinners who by the grace of God have become adopted children of the Most High, born from above to eternal life.

"Come on," the cynical misanthrope down the street cries in protest, "how do you know all that stuff? Where's your proof that heaven exists? You're building castles in the air!"

No, we Christians are not building anything. We simply have the best source of information. We have discovered through our study of the Bible that human life on this earth is not an end in itself; that for us it is a road test, a proving ground, a shakedown cruise, a simulator flight. In response to

God's command, we have become pilgrims just passing through, making a kind of Starbucks stop on earth on our way to our destination.[5]

Such is obedience. It is a foretaste of heaven.

It's true that sometimes the disciplinary expressions in the Bible seem hard to accept. Elisabeth Elliot writes in her newsletter about a young mother who chafed at a verse in Titus (2:5) to the effect that young women of the church should be "keepers at home." The inquirer was answered sympathetically, but Mrs. Elliot did not try to improve on the apostle Paul. She simply told the young mother that in studying God's Word, "obedience always leads finally to joy."

What a beautiful expression! And it's true.

Dr. Ed Wheat, who has written splendid books on married love, confessed that for two years at the beginning of his Christian life he found it hard to love his wife. Then, when he began to take the Bible seriously, he understood that it required just that kind of serious love from him. When he responded, things began to change. He wrote, "As I put the principles of the Bible into practice and I learned really how to love my wife, this became pleasure as well as responsibility. Obedience took on the bright colors of joy!"[6]

The point of this discussion has been to lift obedience out of the category of duty and obligation, and to paint it in those bright and joyful colors. Now we must look at a far more significant aspect of our subject, namely, the obedience of our Lord Jesus Christ Himself to the will of His Father.

"FOR THE JOY..."

Charles Hodge, the great nineteenth-century teacher and scholar at Princeton, wrote that "the obedience of Christ was the righteousness of God."[7] In other words, our Lord's obedience to His Father on the cross did more than just accomplish our rescue. All those trials, jeerings, sufferings, and cruelties that were heaped upon Him, together with His execution as a criminal, actually brought about a change in the moral universe. *Our sins were forgiven!*

Yet while we cheer the victory over death, we remember how distressing was the vicarious sacrifice. When Jesus arrived in Jerusalem over the protest of His disciples, He knew what awaited Him. A feeling of dread is evident in our Lord's prayer in the Garden of Gethsemane, just before His arrest. "Abba, Father," He prayed, "all things are possible for You. Take this cup away from Me; nevertheless, not what I will, but what You will."[8]

As the letter to the Hebrews tells us, this was more than the Son's duty to His Father, a carrying out of paternal orders. It was *"for the joy that was set before Him"* that Jesus *"endured the cross, despising the shame,"*[9] and then sat down at the right hand of the throne of Almighty God.

Joy! Joy at the accomplishment of our redemption from sin and the obtaining of our freedom! Delight at the prospect of returning to His Father and the everlasting joy of heaven!

For us who are Christians, the same beatific prospect is in sight today. Not because of our willingness to be obedient to a "heavenly vision," but because of His willingness to suffer and die and give His life for us in atonement for our sins. Not because of our repentance and confession and obedience, but because of the shed blood of Jesus that thwarted forever the grasp of the evil one and made for us a path to glory.

God Himself, in fact, became our Savior. God Himself became our Redeemer. And God Himself will welcome us one day to that great throne room of the whole creation. Why? Because of the joyful obedience of His Son.

16

THE JOY OF PRAYER

✦

I will...make them joyful in My house of prayer.
—ISAIAH 56:7

*H*i. Abba, Father, it's me. Hi."

Next to salvation in Jesus, prayer is the greatest gift the God who smiles ever gave to the human race. Every week half a trillion prayers are offered up at His heavenly altar. Prayer is the unassailable proof God provides to show that, unlike all other creatures, the Creator made us humans in His own image and likeness. Over the millennia, prayer has become perhaps the one outstanding achievement of human life in its tenure on planet Earth.

But what do all these prayers to God mean? Rees Howells, the great Welsh intercessor, has told us in six startling words. He said, *"The meaning of prayer is answer."*[1] Very well put. There are thousands of books telling us how to pray, but what's the point of any of them if there is no answer? Think of all the prayers of adoration, confession, thanksgiving, supplication, and submission offered every day to God, and then ask, how many requests are filled? How many petitions win a response?

Are *your* prayers answered?

Let me propose a rule of thumb for every Christian: *Because you are God's child, there is no such thing as unanswered prayer.* God always hears you, and He always answers you in one of three different ways—He says YES, or He says NO, or He says WAIT.

If it is Yes, then you are home free. God has blessed you. Sing us a song, cut yourself some pie, and enjoy!

If it is No, then don't argue. Try something else. Maybe God has different plans to bless you and is telling you something.

If it is Wait, then stop praying about it and start trusting. God's timing is perfect. As for His answer—it may not be what you thought you wanted when it comes, but it will be the blessing He wanted.

Have fun!

Rees Howells is right, I am now convinced. Any book on prayer (and I have a stack) should start not with a discussion of our forms and liturgies, nor with the value and importance of prayer, but rather with God Himself, the Giver and Answerer of prayer. And I have a relevant thought to add: *The real joy of prayer is also answer.* Not the enthusiasm we muster in building the altar or digging the trench. Not in erecting a magnificent cathedral of prayer. Not in polishing the phrases of our lectionaries and liturgies. Not in exercising our limbs in a prayer dance or in rewriting the prayers of earlier prayer books.

The joy of prayer comes with the *answer*, when in response to our appeal to the unseen resources of heaven, things happen. Waves are backed up, a fog covers the retreat, stillborn babies suddenly begin to breathe, souls are turned from sin and Satan to Jesus, and unexpected-but-prayed-for "coincidences" occur to change the course of history. Joy comes when after all bold human attempts fail and all glamorous human efforts come to nothing, *God* acts. A little child shuts its eyes and prays for a parent, and the Holy One lifts His finger (so to speak), and Prayer Number 2,345,678,987,654 is suddenly and miraculously answered.

Talk about joy! Talk about jubilation, exultation, unbeliev-ability, gladness of heart, and laughter and tears of joy! There is nothing this side of heaven to match it. And it happens all the time, if the Spirit of prayer is present.

PRAYER IN THE PAST

Let me refresh your memory about some of the great prayer warriors of the ages. Start with Abraham, kneeling at the tere-binth of Mamre. Then Moses, and Elijah and Elisha, Isaiah and Jeremiah, and Hannah, Elizabeth, Mary, Simeon, Anna, and Paul, to name just a few in the Book of Books. Think again about the words of James, the half-brother of the Lord: "You do not *have* because you do not *ask*. You ask and do not receive, because you ask *amiss*....But He gives more grace...The effec-tive, fervent prayer of a righteous man avails much."[2]

Think of the godly men and women who followed the wake of the apostles and took the gospel to the ends of the known earth, by camel caravan, by ship, and on foot. Their principal fuel? Prayer. The early missionaries such as Columba, Kenti-gern, Ninian, and Ansgar prayed the Britons and Celts from druidism to Jesus. Lady Julian of Norwich is still remembered for her delightful style of intercession.[3] God answered the prayers of the Pilgrim fathers and the other Puritans by founding the colonies of North America. What joy that brought to the believers from Britain and Europe who thereby escaped the rampant religious persecution!

In our own land many an unknown saint has taken joy in prayers answered while training children and grandchildren to grow up in the nurture and love of God. God changed my own life forever by attending to the prayers of a quiet Pennsylvania artist-widow who loved Jesus.

It was in 1958 that I met Dr. Nelson Bell, the father of Mrs. Ruth Graham, in San Francisco when Billy Graham held a crusade there. Dr. Bell told me later that he prayed for me every day *by name*. In his home I saw where he did his praying. Do you wonder how an unknown minister and ex-newspaperman could be asked to edit what became the world's most popular Christian magazine, *Decision?* Rees Howells could have told you: "The meaning of prayer is answer."

JOY IN PRAYER?

Another man of God, Ole Kristian Hallesby, was an enor-mous help to me spiritually. He changed me from a prayer worrier to a prayer warrior. This warm, gentle, fervent Norwegian Free Lutheran preacher wrote a book titled *Prayer* early in the twentieth century and it became a bestseller in any number of languages.[4] He asked a key question: "Why do most of us fail so miserably at prayer?" That realistic query goads me today to spin an equally important question: "Why is there so little joy in prayer?"

Stop and think again about all those petitions we human beings keep offering up. How many of them are desperate prayers, weeping prayers, anxious prayers, earnest, sober, godly, sincere, agonizing prayers? Did you ever wonder what you would do with them if you were God? I knew a pastor who would spend hours on his knees shouting to God and pounding his fist on the carpet. No joy there. God knows that my heart goes out to all unhappy seekers who cry out to Him, for I have been there. All I can say is that something is wrong with the prayer wheel. It squeaks.

My Bible tells me that Jesus came bringing us joy and the promise of life abundant. It tells me that His healings brought joy to many and that His own joy did not leave Him even at the crucifixion. We read that His own joy enabled Him to endure the scorning, torture, lashings, and cruel impaling on a cross. It says that Jesus' first word uttered after leaving the tomb empty was "Great joy!"[5] And when He left His disciples and returned to glory, they went back to Jerusalem (read the last verse in Luke) with "great joy." When they reached the other followers of Jesus, they all went into the temple and staged a revival!

Writes Dr. Hallesby, "To move in prayer as though one were in one's element, to pray daily with a willing spirit, with joy, with gratitude and with adoration, is something which is *far beyond* our human capacities and abilities. For this a miracle of God is necessary every day. This miracle consists in receiving the Spirit of Prayer." Here then is the secret. When the Holy Spirit imparts to us the "Spirit of Prayer," then praying ceases to be a burden, a drudge, and a duty, and becomes an exciting venture into the Great Unknown, which is unknown no longer.

Hallesby makes three points: First, we no longer need to think we must help God fulfill our prayer. (So much for the old saw, "The Lord helps those who help themselves.") Second, we are no longer to use our prayers to order God to do our bidding. He will not be compelled. (So much for "Do it, Lord, do it," that is, the wing-it, urgent, command type of prayer.) And third, we need to learn always to pray *in the name of Jesus*. It is, Hallesby says, "the one Name that gives unholy men and women access to a holy God."

His book opened a new vista to me. I saw that prayer could be joyful, even fun. It can be filled with thanksgiving. The idea of prayer as heavy and burdensome duty can be discarded. No longer need the prayer life be limited, restricted, or boxed. Once released, it is as free as the air and is carried on wings of love. Demands cannot stifle it. Pressure cannot restrict it. Worry cannot derail it. Instead, our prayers can be immersed in love by the Holy Spirit and charged with thrills, as new fields of opportunity to serve the Lord are brought to mind.

Charles Finney, the great nineteenth-century evangelist, tells an amusing story of his seeking God in prayer meetings at his church in Adams, New York. It seems he refused to let the people pray for him. He wrote in his memoirs, "I did not see that God answered their prayers. I told them, 'I am conscious that I am a sinner, but I don't see that it will do any good for you to pray for me, for you are continually asking, but you do not receive. You have prayed enough since I began attending to have prayed the devil out of Adams, if there is any virtue in your prayers. But here you are praying on, and complaining still.'"[6]

Every minister has had to suffer through such prayers. At times I have wanted to interrupt with the words, "For heaven's sake, wrap it up. I have other things to do besides listening to this." (You don't have to tell me that is a wrong attitude.) I would be cramped in an uncomfortable position on a hard floor and would have to endure a long-winded description of the problems of someone not present whom I never knew. Quite obviously the supplicator expected no solution, nor was there anything for me to do except to listen in spiritual sympathy—and discomfort. But where were the "joyful noises," the gladness, and the singing? Gone with the wind.

When conversion came to Charles Finney, it came with new life and God's great love and the Joy of the Lord. Dr. Hallesby has a particularly vivid description of the way new life moved into his own soul, but he pictures it as it would happen for anyone:

> Light from above falls into the darkness of the person's soul. Jesus has died for his sins. He is a child of God. He does not need anything besides his Savior. It is as though his heart would burst with joy! He gives thanks, he sings praises and songs of joy to the wonderful God who saves sinners.[7]

Such is the joy of prayer. And did this happen to me, and if so, how? All I can say is, Yes, God answered. A better, more spiritual description of what happens to prayers is found in the fifth chapter of Revelation:

> I looked, and behold…a Lamb.…Now when He had taken the scroll, the four living creatures and the twenty-four elders fell down before the Lamb, *each having a harp, and golden bowls full of incense, which are the prayers of the saints. And they sang a new song, saying: "You are worthy…for You were slain, and have redeemed us to God by Your blood out of every tribe and tongue and people and nation, and have made us kings and priests to our God."*[8]

"Good night, Abba. Thanks a lot."

17

THE JOY OF FRIENDSHIP

❧

Wouldst have a friend,
wouldst know what friend is best?
Have God thy friend, who passeth all the rest.

—THOMAS TUSSER (1524–1580)

From the Bible, we know that God once actually visited the earth. He came in the Person of His Son, Jesus of Nazareth. And what was Jesus doing during His years with us? He was making friends—millions and millions of them, as it has turned out today. Here is what He said about friendships:

> Greater love has no one than this, than to lay down one's life for his friends. You are My friends if you do whatever I command you. No longer do I call you servants,....but I have called you friends....You did not choose Me, but I chose you....The Father Himself loves you, because you have loved Me. [1]

And he added a practical word to spell out friendship in action: "Agree with your adversary quickly." [2]

During His brief ministry on earth, Jesus had no secretarial staff, no administrative team, no personal servants, escorts, or bodyguards. But He had these friends, men and women of God, who made new friends and so built the Christian church. Some of them were unlettered. Some could not read. All of them spoke with a Galilean accent. They were not politically correct. They got into trouble with civil law, religious law, and military law. Some had faith but lacked polish. Some had grasped only part of the gospel that Jesus had taught them, and their faith was weak. But they walked where Jesus walked, and with one exception, they were filled with the Spirit as Jesus was, and the smile of God was upon them.

As the years passed, some of those friends managed to make some historical notes and wrote a few letters and manuscripts. Following the Roman roads through Africa, Asia, and Europe, they created a ministry based on God's friendship for humanity and His great love for His Son Jesus. Those early friends had the joy of knowing their sins were forgiven. They felt the power and love of the Holy Spirit, and they shared it, together with the promise of life everlasting.

Today, as the result of a few friendships with the right Person, the Christian church claims a billion living souls and is looking for more.

If you think I am laboring a point, go through the New Testament and look for Jesus' friends. You will find them among Canaanites, Roman soldiers, Samaritans, invalids, strong men, old people, young children—even Pharisees! Then turn to the book of Romans, chapter 16, and read the list of friends of both sexes made by one man, a Jewish apostle, among Asians, Jews, Maltese, Greeks, Macedonians, Roman rulers, sailors, and tentmakers. What love! What affection! What friendship!

INTIMACY WITH OUR FRIEND

Now, if you are ready, I would like to talk with you as friend to friend. You have picked up this book. Perhaps at the moment you are a single. By your choice or through some circumstance, you are making your way through life alone. Perhaps you lost your mate through death. Perhaps you have never had a mate but would like one. Perhaps you had one but are now divorced. Perhaps, like our Lord, you prefer singlehood. Perhaps you are married but are separated. Or perhaps you are now living in a "safe house" from fear.

You know about me that I am married, but for years I lived as a single in different places—Hawaii, Scotland, Alaska, the Aleutian chain, California, and at sea as a sailor. I know what it's like. Sometimes it's lonely, sometimes it's not. But when you are living on your own, friendships are double blessings.

All this is leading to another question.

Did you ever stop to think that God is longing for your company? Well, He is. There on His great throne, controlling the operation of the universe, He is wishing you would communicate with Him. You may be thinking that I am out of sync and ridiculous to say such things, but stop for a minute. *God made you.* He scooped up some dust, and there you were. (Your HMO would express it differently, but what do they know?) He made you and planted you in your mother's womb, and here you are, drinking coffee perhaps, and reading a book that says this same God who made you is smiling on you and wants to be your Friend. Imagine!

If God is indeed smiling on you and you know it, then He is your Friend already, and that makes you my friend. I realize that because of some immediate, difficult situation, it may be hard for you to absorb all this. In fact, your finger is about to flip the page—but wait. *Wait!*

It's *true* that God likes you. He loves you. In fact, He misses you and would give a lot to hear from you. You make Him smile. He wants to know how things are going with you. Don't tell me that He doesn't have time for you, that He is busy somewhere else. (It's more likely that you don't have time for Him!) But just think about time. The fact is, God invented it. There was no such thing as time until He made it. And He will be glad to make time for you, because you are special to Him.

God's great loving heart longs for intimacy with friends. It doesn't bother Him that you might not happen to have academic qualifications. Why should it? Show me a Bible character who ever had them. Moses? In Egypt, perhaps? But in the wilderness, diplomas and certificates were not much help at finding waterholes, and in heaven they rank even lower. I'm sure our smiling God values the company of all those who believe in Him and love Him, regardless of their status in life. I'm not so sure He is impressed by all the "civilized" noises that reverberate upward from planet Earth to the outposts of His kingdom.

All through the Bible one gathers evidence that the King of kings is not swayed by the endless international social, racial, and moral (not to mention religious) confusion of our daily lives. Instead He seems to wish He could cultivate more warm friends among us. Sometimes I think God would like to attempt an experiment like the genial Caliph Haroun al-Rashid, who would put on a disguise and leave his Baghdad palace in the evenings and walk about town incognito, visiting with his subjects and learning how life was treating them.[3] Then I remember that the Lord Jesus Christ did just exactly that, 2000 years ago.

THE VALUE OF FRIENDSHIP

It's truly amazing what firm friendships can still accomplish in today's world. Friendships cement peace between peoples. Friendships pool resources so that they become available across borders. Friendships aid diplomacy in writing treaties and avoiding wars. They unite tribes and families by replacing quarrels with trust. They provide mutual protection in good times and find ways to survive when times are not so good.

Friendship is God's remedy in overcoming physical difficulties, natural disasters, and human greed, as well as jealousy, enmity, hostility, bitterness, and resentment. When such troubles break out, friendship under God can bring about healing and inspire joy, always assuming that the friendship is stronger than the quarrel.

I believe a case can be made for the statement that *just about everything in the history of the human race that has amounted to anything has been brought about through friendships.* Not necessarily by political leadership or imperial power. Good friendships can be stronger than even nuclear capability, and will certainly do a much better job.

I can think of two personal friends who, by word and deed, radically and permanently changed the direction of my own life and helped me to be established in a saving relationship with Jesus Christ, which caused the God of heaven to smile and send me hightailing on His errands all over the world.

The Apocrypha, a collection of religious writings largely from between the Old and New Testament times, has some interesting thoughts about the value of friendship. The book *Ecclesiasticus,* also called *The Wisdom of Sirach,* is not part of the Bible, but it contains some fascinating observations. One of the best-known passages begins with, "Let us now praise famous men...for they are a great glory to the Lord who created them."[4] I mention it because my own opinion is that the renown of "famous men" is usually based not on their own achievements so much as on the personal friendships they formed earlier in their lifetimes, which guided and steered them toward their renown.

Ben Sirach, the author of those words, was himself aware of the value of such friendships, for he also wrote,

A faithful friend is a strong protection....
A faithful friend is beyond price;
   his value cannot be weighed.
A faithful friend is a life-giving medicine,
   and those who fear the Lord will find it.
The man who fears the Lord will make genuine
   friendships,
   for to him his neighbor is like himself.[5]

"HAVE GOD THY FRIEND"

The wonder and joy of friendship, and even the sorrow of friendship gone awry, bring us back to this: Originally all human friendships were simply joyful icons and reflections of God's primordial friendship with His own creatures. The book of Genesis tells us that after He made man, God decided it was not good for man to be alone. He needed a friend. So out of His own friendship for man, God made another human being and named her woman.[6] Immediately life brightened up, and human joyance entered the garden.

In fact, God in His wisdom has made friendship a key secret to the good life. If you study all the truly great and good things that have happened in human history, whether spiritual or not, look for the strong, quiet friendships behind them that brought those good things into being.

And the simple advice that God has given us—"A man who has friends must himself be friendly"[7]—has always reflected His own steadfast relations with humanity. He is friendly! After the Old Testament tells us of the creation of the first friendship, it goes on to say that both Abraham and Moses were on "friendly" terms with God; but the New Testament goes further and tells us that God yearns to be Friend to the whole human race.

It was because "God so loved the world" that He sent His Son to us. As the apostle Paul wrote to Timothy, "God our Savior...desires all men to be saved and to come to the knowledge of the truth."[8] No matter how glorious is His awesome majesty as the Bible describes it, those who know Him say that joyful, intimate personal relationship is still the essence of His nature. And ever since He created us, Almighty God, the Lord of the universe, has proved again and again to be the best Friend the human race has ever had.

Thoughts on Friendship

Friendship in the Family

One of the most badly needed friendships of the new millennium is between the generations. A dangerous gap is developing between teenagers and their parents, not to speak of their grandparents. The generation gap is social, musical, political, educational, cultural, recreational, legal, and sexual.

In a real sense the gap has always been there. My father was 47 years old when I was born, and growing up I was utterly convinced that we lived in different worlds. For 40 years he was good to me, but I was bitter toward him. The self will always keep grievances uppermost and well-fed.

Not until I reached my late forties and Dad was in his early nineties did God graciously reach down and seal our hearts together in the beautiful love of Jesus. Only friendship like this, rooted in God's love, will close the gap—in the twenty-first century no less than in any other.

FRIENDSHIP MAKES THIS LIFE RICH

This world is not my home—
I'm just a-passing through.

This sentiment is simply expressed but biblically accurate. I agree with it, and look forward with the author of the letter to the Hebrews to the homeland that God has prepared in heavenly country for those who love Him (Hebrews 11:13-16). After nine decades here on earth, I cannot buy Robert Louis Stevenson's fatuous nursery rhyme:

The world is so full of a number of things,
I'm sure we should all be as happy as kings.

But somewhere in between here and our homeland there ought to be room for a Christian to say that he has deeply enjoyed living on this globe, if for no other reason than the rich friendships he has made while "a-passing through."

CREATION'S FRIENDSHIP

There is an aspect of friendship on this earth that we don't express very often. It is a friendship with the earth itself. We are earth people, creatures designed by God for this planet. It in turn is designed for us—and I sincerely wish scientists would stop trying to get people to leave it in some contraption or other.

Right here on terra firma we are blessed with so much that we have come to love: the clean air, the blue sky, the shining sea, the bright flowers, the rolling hills and valleys, the waterfalls, the fruitfulness of trees and bushes, the changing of the seasons, the goodness of the soil, the color of jewels, the singing of the birds, the affection of pets—so much to enjoy, so much for which to thank God our Creator!

In fact, the whole globe is so filled with such delights that I find it hard to express its variety and charm; yet in a lifetime I have seen so little of it. Christians have a right to regard the earth as a beautiful place, created by the supreme Artist for His own joy and pleasure and out of friendship for His creatures.

FRIENDSHIP IN HIGH PLACES

I know the risks and dangers in mountain climbing, but I have never sought to prove anything, just to enjoy the mountains. They have been such friends to so many people. I would like to say a word of thanksgiving for them: Fuji, Shasta, Lassen, Whitney, Tulik in the Aleutians, Halfdome, San Gorgonio, San Jacinto, Pikes Peak, Mauna Kea, Washington, Lincoln, Monroe, Ayers Rock, Giza Pyramid, Katoomba, Rothorn—yes, and the Washington Monument. These and many more felt the touch of my feet and responded with a quiet challenge. I bask today in the memory of their friendships.

THE MOST INCLUSIVE FRIENDSHIP

I grew up in a home where racism did not exist. Before I left high school, my father had circled the globe four times and crossed the Atlantic in steamships nineteen times on missions of charity. As children we were taught that friendship toward all peoples was God's will for us.

I have been privileged to visit with Aboriginal Australians, Pakistani Muslims, Egyptian Muslims, Alaskan Eskimos, North American Indians, Russians, Taiwanese natives, Samoan natives, Hawaiian natives, Japanese Nisei and Issei, Orientals, Indonesians, Hindus, black South Africans, black Americans, Brazilians, Colombians, and New Zealand Maoris, and found them all beautiful people and eager for friendship.

For Jesus there was no race problem, there was friendship and joy.

I follow Jesus.

OUR FUTURE WILL TRIUMPH THROUGH HIM

18
WHEN GOD STOPPED SMILING

All aboard for Blanket Bay
Won't come back till the break of day.
Roll him 'round in his trundle white sheet
Till you can't see his dear little feet.
Bless Mama, bless Papa, and sail away
All aboard for Blanket Bay!

*S*ongs our mother used to sing to my brother Lincoln and me at bedtime, under a smiling God, can convey perhaps better than adjectives and adverbs what life was like 85 or so years ago—and believe me, it was *totally* different!

For example, listen to this childhood litany we loved to repeat: "Engine, coal car, mail car, coach, dining car, sleeping car, observation car." That, in a word, was a *train.* "Whooooooo, whooooooo, whoo, whoooooooo!" That was a train whistle we heard every night. A locomotive was a puffer-belly with a cowcatcher that caught cows, goats, sheep, sometimes children and drunks. A caboose was—well, a caboose. If you don't understand, rest assured that we kids did. It was the Age of Trains.

That age possessed its own flavor, and so did the circumstances of my young life, before they were broken into so rudely and unsmilingly by later school experiences. And this flavor is perhaps best communicated by a few stories of my growing-up years.

157

Ours was a big family in a big house. We lived in a suburb of Boston, Massachusetts. We were churchfolk, attending the First Congregational Church of Wellesley Hills. Prayer, Bible verses, children's tunes, Sunday school, the whole Christian ball of wax was ours. We memorized the Beatitudes, 1 Corinthians 13, and several Psalms. But don't imagine that all that made brother Lincoln and me model children.

Father was an Important Person and was away lecturing about his dog-team trek across Alaska, but when he was at home our atmosphere changed dramatically, with two additions: family prayers and spankings. For prayers we all knelt at chairs in the parlor (I got the footstool), and being the youngest, I had to start. What I communicated to God is (thankfully) known only to Him, but my silent prayers, like Augustine's, were for deliverance from spankings.

So what brought on the strap? Well, we discovered that Mother "charged" things at Mr. DeFazio's grocery store, so we began charging chewing gum and LifeSavers and a delicious molasses candy we called "monkey candy." That was stopped with a strap. Then we found that street workers had deposited a barrel of hot tar on our street. Since chewing gum was out, we began chewing hot tar, and it did nothing good to our teeth or to our backsides.

When winter snows came, we got out our sleds and dragged them up a hill to slide down. Then we discovered something much more fun and a lot less work, namely, hitching our sleds to the milkman's delivery wagon. His gallant nag then did the dragging, taking us on a tour of the village. Oh, we easily found wrong things to do, and the spankings ceased not.

I, a year younger than brother Lincoln, proved ingenious at pretending to be childish, innocent, and dumb, so Lincoln would usually be blamed for whatever we did wrong. I came across a jingle recently that helps explain our relationship:

The rain it raineth everywhere
Upon the Just and Unjust Fella,
But more upon the Just, they say,
For the Unjust has the Just's umbrella.

Lincoln was my umbrella.

On one marvelously exciting day we went to the silent movies and saw Charlie Chaplin's famous war comedy *Shoulder Arms*. On another day Mother took us to Natick on a streetcar, and we saw the old oak tree where our ancestor on our mother's side, John Eliot (1604–1670), pioneer missionary to the Indians of New England, preached to his flocks while sitting on a very large limb, using the Bible he had translated into Algonquian.

Soon after my eighth birthday our family packed up and climbed aboard the Wolverine Express of the New York Central Railroad, starting thus a cross-country move to California. We were deprived of the luxury of the dining car because Mother had brought along a huge basket full of sandwiches, which we munched day by day across the fruited plains.

Father joined us in Kansas where he was lecturing on the Chautauqua circuit. A week later an unforgettable moment occurred when the journey resumed. We waited at midnight, I with heart in mouth, on the right-of-way at a mid-Kansas grade crossing, as a signalman walked out on the tracks and flagged down the huge, whistling, roaring Overland Limited express train. Why? Just so our family could climb aboard the monster and head for San Francisco.

In California we moved into an 11-room house in North Berkeley and began a new life. I was promoted to high fourth grade, made new friends, and dropped my Boston accent. On Sundays Lincoln and I bicycled downtown to the First Congregational Church, while Mother and sister Monica rode the streetcar. Father was usually away somewhere, raising money for some cause.

Berkeley was a quiet, conservative, academic town that voted for Herbert Hoover—quite different from its reputation today. Businessmen rode the electric trains to the end of the Oakland "mole" and ferried across the bridgeless San Francisco Bay to "the City." At age 12 I joined the Boy Scouts and before my fourteenth birthday received the Eagle Scout badge. At Berkeley High School I learned to my chagrin that I was too small to participate in athletics. (On the 130-lb. football squad I spent virtually the entire season on the bench as fourth-string quarterback.) I decided to become a writer. In 1928 my grades were adequate to enroll me across town as a freshman student at the University of California.

Then, with a suddenness that shocked me, three things occurred that upset the even tenor of my adolescence. A college fraternity surprised me with a pledge pin. I found a copy of Sinclair Lewis' book *Elmer Gantry* in my father's library and read it. And the University assigned me to a required course called Philosophy 5-A.

The fraternity was a whole new world with a whole new language, in which parental and church influences were either forgotten or ignored. The "bull session" replaced prayers. Sorority teas replaced Sunday-school picnics. Ribald songs replaced the church hymnbook. Profanity replaced clean speech. Prohibition reigned, and homemade bathtub gin replaced the 15-cent milkshakes of high-school days. I grew up fast.

Sinclair Lewis was a brilliant but tortured Midwestern writer who despised the young "muscular Christians" of his acquaintance. He also fantasized the hypocrisy of the clergy by making the Reverend Elmer Gantry a thoroughgoing rascal and lecher. His novel stated that everything Jesus taught He had "borrowed" from earlier rabbis and that He added nothing new. Thus was my Savior reduced to just another guy. I had no deep religious interest at the time, but what I read in *Gantry* shocked me, as I still had vestiges of my childhood love for Jesus.

The philosophy course in which I was enrolled assigned us the writings of Lucretius, an ancient Roman poet-philosopher who lived a century before Christ (approximately 95–55 B.C.). His lengthy poem "On the Nature of Things" *(De Rerum Natura)* succeeded in completely devastating me and destroyed my belief in everything supernatural.[1]

Not that Lucretius attacked God Himself; he knew nothing of our true Lord, but he ridiculed the whole pagan pantheon of gods and goddesses, declaring that no one believed in them any more. He also repudiated the idea of immortality, asserting that the soul itself died with the body and both returned to "atoms." He defined death as "the end," which meant *that it is nothing.* But, he added calmly, so what? "Is there aught in this that wears an aspect of gloom? Is it not more untroubled than any sleep?"

I got his message. There is no heaven, no life beyond this one, no God of love, and no Lord Jesus. The sky is empty, but there is nothing at all to worry about. Churchgoing is an enormous waste of time. Religion is a fantasy. Prayer is nonsense. Even love is stupid. As for my early childhood vow to be "clean and sweet for Jesus' sake," that was now ridiculous.

What a shocking effect upon the soul! I had no defense. By now I had moved into the fraternity house. On my next visit to my parents, I informed them that I no longer believed in God.

All unknown to me, my Lord had stopped smiling upon me.

How did I survive all this change? Regarding the fraternity experience, it took years to sift out the good points from the bad. In many ways the fraternity actually helped me to grow up. It exposed me to adult life. It did not teach me to do stupid things; I made those decisions myself. It did provide me often with a fraternal bed on which to sleep during the Depression, long after I had graduated.

The effect of the book *Elmer Gantry* was not easy to overcome. Not until I studied Sinclair Lewis himself did I realize he was writing out of his own sour experience of rejection by his peers as well as by churches—in part perhaps because of his homely looks. He certainly took pleasure in making Gantry a sham preacher, thus objectifying his bitter feelings. His anger in the book was the skillful product of a rejected persona.

Even more serious was the damage done to my naive soul by the philosopher Lucretius. Decades passed before I learned the truth about the man and realized that he, like Sinclair Lewis, was spewing out hostility because of his social rejection. No doubt the university thought that Lucretius would make us students "think," but for me the man's unbelief created uncertainty and sadness. Life lost its meaning. These were the years of the Great Depression, and wherever I went in my young newspaper career—Hawaii, Alaska, California— I was lonely and frustrated. My trouble was not just with God, but with everything—jobs (few), girls (distant), friendships (wrong), my writing (rejects), and money (none).

Peace finally arrived years later when I came across the following description of Lucretius in a journal kept by Jerome, the translator of the Vulgate Bible, who lived in Rome in the fourth century A.D. (His source seems to have been the second-century Roman historian Suetonius.) Jerome wrote, "Titus Lucretius the poet...was rendered insane by a love philtre [by drinking a supposed magic potion to induce love] and, after writing some books during periods of lucidity, which Cicero emended [edited], he died by his own hand in the forty-third year of his life."[2]

What a discovery! It told me all I needed to know about this ancient infidel who had so cleverly obliterated my childish faith. "Sex obsession…mental collapse…suicide." Hardly a good source to consult about the "nature of things." As Emerson once remarked, "What you are stands over you the while, and thunders so that I cannot hear what you say to the contrary."

By the time I finally learned that lesson, I was married and had become a Christian and a minister. Life was still very difficult, but it seemed God was about ready to make a move.

19
EPIPHANY AT WATERLOO STATION

❦

Every man meets his Waterloo at last.

—WENDELL PHILLIPS

*T*he telephone rang at my modest church in south Berkeley, California, on a day in April, 1954. "This is Margaret Donaldson, Dr. Munger's secretary."

Robert Boyd Munger and I had been classmates at Berkeley High School and later at "Cal." He then attended Moody Bible Institute and Princeton Seminary, and was now pastoring Berkeley's largest church. At the time he was ranked the outstanding preacher of the gospel on the Pacific Coast and had become to me more than a friend; he was my mentor.

"Dr. Munger is back from his ministry in India," Margaret said, "and he brought with him a reel of film about the Billy Graham crusade in London, where he stopped over. He thought some of you pastors would like to see it."

"I would."

"We will be showing it at ten o'clock tomorrow."

"Thanks. I'll be there."

What a relief! For a few minutes tomorrow I wouldn't have to think about the leak in the church roof, or the family that planned to leave the church, or the children's sermon for next Sunday. Next morning I met a few evangelical pastor friends in a social parlor of Dr. Munger's church. A Bell and Howell projector was threaded with the 16-millimeter sound film, the shades were drawn, and we were off in spirit to "old Blighty."

What we saw during the next few minutes so fascinated me that my memory of it is nearly as clear today as it was half a century ago. We watched Billy Graham and his team in black-and-white, arriving aboard the HMS *Queen Mary* at Southampton, England, and being greeted by British churchmen and dignitaries. We watched them seated aboard a train to London, where Billy was to preach nightly for 12 weeks in North London's Harringay Arena.

The next scene remains especially memorable. We saw the huge Waterloo railway station in the city of London packed with joy-filled Christians, there to welcome Billy Graham, Cliff Barrows, George Beverly Shea, Grady Wilson, and others of the American team. We saw smiles and hand-wavings and heard laughter and cheers and shouting and clapping, together with the impromptu singing of "Glory for Me" and "What a Friend We Have in Jesus" and other gospel hymns. A commentator told us the crowd was so large that the platform ticket machines gave out. Extra police had to be summoned, and the singing was lost in the sound of sirens as more police arrived. However, from a raised point the song leader, Cliff Barrows, continued to lead the milling concourse in verse after happy verse. There was an official greeting from the crusade committee, and then slowly, very slowly, the visitors made their way through the crush of humanity to the waiting cars, shaking hands and hugging all the way.

To my mind the whole scene became a kind of epiphany: not so much a vision of heaven as a perception of the essential meaning of true Christianity; or perhaps even better, an intuitive grasp of what was real. I seemed to see in a flash how Jesus Himself was surrounded by an equally enthusiastic crowd celebrating on the shore of the Sea of Galilee while He preached the good news of the kingdom of God.

His lighthearted words seemed to float through my mind: "Take heart. Be of good cheer, I have overcome the world. I have come that you might have life, and have it abundantly."[1]

Jesus was evidently determined to bring the kingdom of God not just to the synagogues or to the religious folk, but to everybody. That is why He chose to follow the shoreline of Galilee, rather than limiting Himself to the interiors of buildings. His message was aimed at the entire human population, both then and now. That would include Westminster Abbey, St. Paul's Cathedral, Yankee Stadium—and Waterloo Station.

I saw in that reel of film a spiritual force at Waterloo Station that was greater than political power and more effective than warfare. The Holy Spirit "took over" the place and so filled the people that they were in a rare mood. What was it that helped create such a remarkable scene? It was the Joy of the Lord! As the prophet Zechariah had said prophetically centuries earlier, "This is the Word of the Lord…: 'Not by might nor by power, but by My Spirit,' says the LORD."[2]

As I sat in Bob Munger's church, I couldn't help reflecting on my own beloved south Berkeley congregation and the empty pews down front that stared at me on Sunday mornings. It came upon me in a rush: "This is it! This is the real gospel of Jesus, the glad tidings, the bringing of great love and great joy and great peace to the people. This is not a freak scene on a special occasion. What I am watching is Jesus in action, and what Jesus promised for every day: *Joy. Gladness of spirit. The enjoyment of life together in the Presence of the Lord. Mutual help. Work made easy. Play made jubilant. Life in Christ forever! Glory!"*

It seemed that Waterloo, the big old London train depot, had become a setting for God to reveal His joy factor, that is, the power of His mighty love to bring smiles and good cheer. The atmosphere itself was an elixir strong enough to heal human troubles and hurts. The people seemed to reflect the confident faith that in Christ we are victors over death, and that to know Him is actually to know grace, love, exultation, and merriment—and oh, how I wanted that joy!

I went back to my church convinced that the Joy of the Lord is a reality. It is a crown of delight for the virtues of piety, trust, and obedience. It is a fresh environment, so to speak, something that our Lord Jesus Christ brought with Him from heaven—an inexplicable, overwhelming gladness at being alive. God reigns! God's Spirit is working in human hearts! Believers are kicking up their heels! Waterloo station gave us a shivering awareness of eternity. I saw the Holy Spirit lifting up human spirits in ways that can only be expressed by joyous human laughter. But how to capture it?

Years would pass before the answer fully penetrated my soul. What I retained after watching the film was mainly that God was real and present here today in radiance and glory. He did not die in the days of Oliver Cromwell, as Thomas Carlyle hinted that He did. God is not "out there someplace" or "down the tube." The unbelief of my college days was finally crowded out for good and all, and for the first time since childhood, I began to feel the reality of God's nearness, as I had back in Massachusetts when my mother sat listening to my whispered bedtime promises to my heavenly Father.

More thrilling scenes appeared on that black-and-white film. We saw Billy Graham addressing some of the crowds that packed the 11,000-seat Harringay Arena from January through March. Night after night they came to hear and respond to the gospel of Christ—some of them singing hymns in the "Underground" subway trains. When the invitation was given to come to Christ, much to the astonishment of some of the clergy present, people surged forward to the altar by the hundreds to commit their lives to their Lord.

Then we watched the events at a children's rally in the huge Wembley Stadium, filled to capacity by English youngsters.

They waved, whooped, and jumped up and down as Roy Rogers, the "King of the Cowboys," rode his trick horse "Trigger" around the running track, and his wife Dale Evans Rogers taught the promises of God and the love of Jesus over the loudspeaker.

In the final scene on the film, Billy Graham appeared in the pulpit of a packed London church, where he dealt with some of the sharp criticisms that had been appearing in the metropolitan press. Over and over the newspapers had expressed their objections to his presence: "He comes from a country that has had Christianity for 300 years, to try to convert us who have had Christ for 1900 years!"

I remember exactly that point in the film when Billy made his reply to the English people. He said, "We did not come here to save you. We did not come to reform you. We came at the invitation of the churches of London to preach the unsearchable riches of Jesus Christ to the people of Britain."

Those well-chosen, inspired words proved reassuring to the listeners in London. But I, in my chair in California, was more deeply touched by two verses Billy then quoted from the King James Bible to undergird his statements. One was from Psalm 27:8: "When Thou saidst, Seek ye my face; my heart said unto thee, Thy face, LORD, will I seek." The other was from Jeremiah 29:13: "Ye shall seek me, and find me, when ye shall search for me with all your heart." What a challenge, and did I ever need it!

The epiphany at Waterloo Station, thanks to that Bell & Howell projector, eventually brought about changes in my church, chiefly through the Holy Spirit as He renewed my own spirit. What I had to face during the ensuing days was that the crowds at Waterloo sparkled as our congregation didn't, because we didn't know how. The Waterloo crowd enjoyed their fellowship with God and each other. They were charmed and filled with anticipation. Scripture was coming alive. The love of God, as Paul said, was "poured out into our hearts by the Holy Spirit given to us."[3] The authentic gospel of Jesus Christ invariably brings with it the prospect of the joy of His salvation. To which I would like to add Francis Schaeffer's perceptive comment: "God means Christianity to be fun."[4]

Here then was a fresh outlook on life for me to seek and obtain. As a young newspaperman working on four different dailies, I had covered much that did not exactly sparkle, from traffic accidents and murder trials to writing the "20 Years Ago" column. Later as a student pastor I had enjoyed praying with people, ministering to their needs, preaching, and working at youth camps; but at my first California church I was forced to spend far too much time wrestling with problems emerging from a stubborn monthly budget and a salary of $4000 per annum.

It happened two months later that Billy Graham paid a brief visit to San Francisco and preached in the city's Civic Auditorium. Like other Bay Area pastors, I filled up my car with church members and drove them across the Bay to hear him. An usher spotted me outside the building and escorted me to the platform to join a chorus of 50 singing ministers. Then after the service ended I set out to try to find my passengers. Finally I located their seats, but they were empty. It seems all my people had gone forward to recommit their lives to Jesus Christ!

It is absolutely incredible what God can do when the Joy of the Lord begins to seep into the life of a church. Four years later Billy Graham came back to San Francisco for a seven-week evangelistic crusade. At that time I was pastoring a lively east Oakland church. As we prayed for Billy to bring revival to the churches of the Bay Area, the congregation began to respond. Elders and young people and couples and singles traveled across the bay to attend the meetings in the Cow

Palace. Our church chartered a daily bus; the driver was converted. We sang in the·choir. We ushered. We counseled. And back at the church, our Wednesday evening prayer meetings began to glow.

And then the following year, at Billy Graham's invitation, I boarded a Pan American transpacific flight and headed for Melbourne, Australia to join his team and to become editor of a new magazine he was planning, to be called *Decision*.

Thank you, Waterloo station.

20

FACING THE REAL QUESTION: GOD

❧

Truth is so obscured in these times,
and falsehood so established,
that unless one loves the truth,
he cannot know it.

—BLAISE PASCAL (1623–1662)

*R*ecently it was my pleasure to meet Ken Blue, a minister-author who has done God's church a favor by writing books which expose the way some churches use their power and influence to hurt people. He has achieved a national reputation in this field. Ken is a genuine scholar and the active pastor of Foothills Church in San Diego. His research has exposed a busy commerce of satanic activity by pseudoreligious types that is eating away at the gains of the gospel and is severely damaging the reputation of Christianity in America.

When I encounter stories of cruelty, hypocrisy, cheating, and extortion that involve church people, I have no trouble laying my finger on the real issue. These perpetrators of wrongdoing simply do not *know God* and never will know Him unless there is a radical spiritual change in their lives. While some are "psychos" and publicity seekers, others are deliberate frauds who prey on unsuspecting Christians. Such mountebanks and swindlers treat the word "God" as meaningless jabberwocky.

How such people worm their way into religious circles is an ongoing mystery. After all, Jesus warned His disciples that they should be "wise as serpents and harmless as doves."[1] As for the hypocrites, Pascal said that "one never does evil so completely and cheerfully as when he does it from religious conviction."[2] Such a religious conviction—without the God of love and the love of God—can quickly explode into a firestorm of cruelty and terror.

Twenty years ago or so I concluded that the sovereign majesty of Almighty God (that is, the awareness of God Himself) cut little ice among churchgoers, no matter what the denomination's theological position might be. I attended one Sunday morning church service in which neither God nor Jesus were referred to in the sermon, and it was *not* a liberal gathering. That was extreme; but it is not extreme to state that God the Father, the Creator, the Redeemer, the God of the Bible, the great Object of our worship, seems to be "taken for granted," thus becoming more or less irrelevant to the life of the church.

That conviction motivated me to write a book, *A Thirst for God,* which drew letters that made me feel that it had touched a tender spot. In the book I simply raised the same questions that the psalmists were always raising in their day. Over and over they kept asking, "God, God, God, where are You? Are you real? Why don't You speak to us? How can You let things go on like this? You have neglected us. Don't You care anything about us any more?"

I would not have dared to invade that field if God had not spoken to me before I started to write in a way that penetrated deeply into my soul. It brought a spillage of joy that brimmed my empty cup. I learned at last what it meant to be filled with the Holy Spirit. He poured the love of God into my heart[3], and He has never ever stopped doing it. He started the joybells ringing, and they have never quit, even in pain.

It all came fast. The cross became my theology. The Bible became my favorite book. Prayer became a love tryst. Instead of my life being a disappointment, it became a holiday picnic. My spiritual "growth" shrank several inches around the middle. I even tried to push my ego into a back seat. It was like rediscovering God. Sure, the devil is still around, making problems and yelling at me, "So what?" But God is in charge, and He offers good solutions.

Hoping to find kindred spirits, I recently asked the readers of my monthly magazine column to send me examples of how the Joy of the Lord had touched their lives.

Nancy Bayless wrote, "Often in my 75 years I've wanted to watch a hibiscus open. They do it with delicate swiftness, so that I miss the moment. Recently on a spring morning I went out to watch the phenomenon and became enthralled with the moist coolness of the dew-drenched grass on my bare feet. I saw the glory of God's sunrise and felt the marvel of being alive. I stretched my arms out wide, and turning around, saw that my hibiscus had done the same. God smiled at me as I gently touched its velvet texture and went inside to start my devotions."

Betty Chapman Plude wrote, "Growing up in the church, I never heard that I could have Christ in my heart. During the week I attended choir practice, which imprinted the majesty of the hymns on my very being. It was God's way of giving me a glimpse of His true joy. The hymns comforted me when the not-so-good circumstances stormed into my life. Today when bad things happen I say, 'Thank You, Lord, for filling me with Your love, peace, and joy.' The praise songs of today and the hymns whirl in my heart with hope and thanksgiving."

Dr. Michael Suozzi wrote, "I grew up in the Italian Catholic tradition and left home when I enlisted in the Army. Returning, I entered Columbia University. I did not attend church except at Easter and Christmas, but in class I would wonder, Why did these teachers hate Jesus Christ with such fury?

"I would walk down Amsterdam Avenue and enter the Episcopal Cathedral of St. John the Divine. In late winter afternoons no visitors were there. I would think over where my life was going. Would I ever have the guts to translate what I believed about Jesus Christ into action? One afternoon I wandered into a side chapel where the tomb of Bishop Henry Potter stood along with an effigy of the old man. An inscription I had not noticed before attracted my attention:

CHAMPION OF RIGHTEOUSNESS AND TRUTH.
SOLDIER AND SERVANT OF JESUS CHRIST.

"Filled with sudden joy, I said out loud, 'Yes. That is all there is.' I left the chapel a Christian. I had earned my Ph.D. in record time, but now I had the joy of living and teaching as a Christian. Often I came to the end of my economic rope, but the grace of God was there, and I kept going. Was it worth all this? 'Fear not' is our Savior's injunction, and His word is true. It was God's plan for me. That is the answer."

The Joy of the Lord is a joy unknown in worldly circles. Sex, romance, travel, entertainment, ambition, all the things that the world and its pals, the media, pursue so frantically, pale beside the natural gladness of knowing God as He really is, the God who smiles. How does one describe it? How does one capture this breath of fragrance blown in from another world, the sudden rush of ecstatic tidings, the awareness that we belong to God and are God's, the One who reigns in truth and righteousness? I don't know. Sometimes I forget what my denominational standing is, the way a soldier forgets the pain of his wounds when he is reunited with his loved ones. All I know is that like the psalmist, I am going to the altar of God, my joy and my delight.[4]

Many earnest followers who sincerely honor Jesus Christ are still having difficulty finding God. The Holy Spirit seemingly has not yet manifested Himself in their lives. They act like and look like fine church pillars, but God is still not real to them, and He certainly is not smiling on them. They are having trouble seeing, feeling, understanding, and knowing their Maker. Sometimes they complain that He seems so invisible, so unreal, so "unscientific." They come to church with their devout wives or husbands, but they don't really pray with their spouses or the congregation because they haven't figured out to whom they are praying.

I love these people dearly, for I was one of them. So I have put together a chapter for them that tells its own story. I have placed a human being in a situation that is as tight as one can make it, with a God as remote as I can draw Him, and have used it to the best of my ability to illustrate the New Testament teaching as to how God shows Himself, how He accomplishes His will, and how He *works*.

So now we will raise the questions again: "Who is God... where is He...is He real...how can I find Him...where is the joy?"

Turn the page.

21

WHEN LIFE TUMBLES IN

You are God my stronghold [fortress].
Why have You rejected me?
Why must I go about mourning,
Oppressed by the enemy?

—PSALM 43:2 NIV

*L*et's suppose there is a particular fortress standing on a granite cliff that rises a thousand feet above the ocean. Its walls are like the Chateau d'If, impregnable. The castle towers are veiled in clouds and mist. Its facade looks forbiddingly out to sea. From the narrow beach below the fortress it appears to be devoid of life. The sheer cliffs on either side of the beach project out into the depths of the water so that the beach itself has no access. The ocean tide is rising, and soon the beach will be under several feet of water.

This is a picture of God, "my fortress."[1] There is a wonderful sense in which God appears to us as a fortress. He is solid, dependable, immutable, firm, impregnable. He will never be captured or overcome. Yet He stands against the sky like a fortress, somber, austere, impenetrable—and silent. He does not speak to us. As a result we feel like the psalmist, rejected. God seems to be a million miles away.

Let's assume you are a shipwreck survivor who was washed up on the beach, barefoot. You are virtually exhausted by your close escape from death. Night is approaching. You have no food, no water, no ammunition, no climbing gear, no flashlight, nothing and no one to help you. The beach is littered with useless rubble. There are no boats, and the surf waves are too high to negotiate by swimming. If there is any way off the beach, you have no idea where it is.

You try to examine the cliffs in the dim light to see if there are any cracks, any footholds, any chimneys. You stumble over what look like human bones. The waves are now beginning to wash over your feet. It does not appear that you can remain much longer where you are. Should you choose not to move, things will just get worse. You ask yourself, *how did I get into this strait?* You think, *perhaps if I beat my fists against the cliff it will relieve my frustration.*

As it grows darker, you notice that far up on the cliffs there seems to be a light in the castle. It is hard to make out because the rain has started, but you feel sure something is up there in that fortress.

Your bare foot touches something, and you reach down to pick it up. It turns out to be a small, dirty, watersoaked, leather-bound New Testament. You try to read it, but the words are too tiny. It causes you to reflect: *Two new things have happened.* You have seen a light up in the castle, and you have found a copy of Scripture. These are signs, perhaps? Certainly they are better than beating your fists against the cliff. But does it mean that somehow God is aware of you, that He is looking down upon your predicament? If so, what is He going to do about it? What can He do? You are becoming very tired.

Perhaps there is something you can do. Instead of complaining, why not accept your situation as an opportunity for positive development and growth?[2] After all, it was not God who spoke of rejection, it was the psalmist. Rejection may be purely a human subjective impression. The book! Even if you can't read the words in the little Testament, you can pray. Pray to God. Ask Him for help...That leads you to think back over your life, trying to remember when it was you last sent up a prayer. You wonder whether prayers ever work. The water is rising. You have to do something. So you pray.

But that is just the trouble. There is no word from God. Like the fortress, He is silent. You open your eyes and look up. If only someone up there would speak or wave a sign. But nothing!

Wearily you look again at the deteriorating situation on the beach. Then—but wait! You see something. It is a tiny light flickering in the distance, at the far end of the beach. Apparently it is moving, but is it coming your way? It is a small light, a torch, and it now definitely seems to be slowly making its way toward you.

Now the wind gives a final burst and dies away, and you begin to hear something far up on the cliff that sounds like— it can't be, but it sounds like—music! As you begin to cry, the music becomes louder. It is a song being sung from far up, a strange song. You hear the words:

> He was despised and rejected by men,
> a man of sorrows, and familiar with suffering.
> Like one from who men hide their faces
> he was despised, and we esteemed him not.
> Surely he took up our infirmities
> and carried our sorrows,
> yet we considered him stricken by God,
> smitten by him, and afflicted.
> But he was pierced for our transgressions,
> he was crushed for our iniquities;
> the punishment that brought us peace was upon him,
> and by his wounds we are healed.[3]

By this time the light has approached quite near to you, and you can vaguely make out a figure walking, or rather wading. You see it is a man clothed in a homespun robe. A wave recedes, and you see He is barefoot like you. He is bearded, with long hair, and He has a familiar look as He comes toward you. Lines on His face show evidence of suffering, but now He is smiling. There is joy on His countenance. Despite the chill in the air, a warm feeling spreads through your body; it is as if you are meeting with an old friend. You want to stay near Him, to feel the touch of His strong hand. He waves, and for the first time you notice His hands.

Your tiredness is gone as He greets you. The frenetic anxiety over your condition has vanished, and your calm is restored. You are not minding a thing, not your wet clothes, not even the grim look of that huge high rock.

Now the Man is beckoning you toward the base of the steep cliff. As you draw near it seems to you the vast rock is more forbidding than ever. By the light of your Friend's torch, you thread your way to the base of the mighty fortress. So complete is the darkness that you cannot see it, but you can feel the smooth wall with your hands. Your Guide is now flashing His light about, and you are astonished to see that He has located a narrow cleft in the rock. He looks at you and seems to smile, then turns and leads the way inside.

As you follow Him it occurs to you that you may never know the full mystery of that fortress; its massiveness, its silences, its recesses. The Bible says that God is indeed a high fortress, the rock of truth. He is a bastion, and bastions don't fluctuate. God is steadfast, indestructible, imperishable. But if right now you cannot fathom the mysteries of the fortress, nothing is lost. *You don't need to know everything about the Almighty, for into the obscure shadows has come a Man with a light.* He is like you and me, one of us, and yet He obviously knows what we do not know. For when you followed Him, He led you off the beach, out of the hopeless circumstances of your life, and into the shelter of His Father, the fortress. You are saved! Delivered!

This is your Friend, Jesus Christ, the best friend our stiff-necked and perverse human race has ever had. He is the Son of the God who smiles, the fortress God, believe it or not. He is the Paraclete[4] who comes alongside us and stands up for us and pleads our cause, and takes our place and bears our iniquity and delivers us from death and hell and saves our souls forever.

Would you like to get off the beach? Would you like to find a place of refuge, a shelter from the forces of wickedness? Then follow Jesus into the cleft in the rock. That's where I went one gloomy day. Yes, I have been on that dreary beach—but do you know what I found in the cleft? (This is unbelievable.) A warm, well-furnished reception area with plenty of towels and sandals, plus clothing, and an express elevator waiting to take me up.

But now you are again alone, for Jesus has gone back to the beach to look for someone else. The elevator is busy. As you wait for it, you open the New Testament and find the letter of James: "Consider it pure joy, my brothers, whenever you face trials of many kinds, because you know that the testing of your faith develops perseverance...Blessed is the man who perseveres under trial, because when he has stood the test, he will receive the crown of life that God has promised to those who love him."[5]

The elevator is now waiting for you. Jesus has shown you the way to God, and it's time to come aboard. Listen! There is that music again. But this time there is a joyful, exultant note. Someone is singing, "All hail the power of Jesus' name..."

22

THE JOY OF FAITHFULNESS

❧

I have fought a good fight,
I have finished my course,
I have kept the faith.

—PAUL (2 TIMOTHY 4:7 KJV)

The life in Christ is not a 100-meter dash, nor is it a mile or two-mile run. Rather it is a marathon. You will remember that the marathon distance (based on the ancient victory run from the plains of Marathon to Athens, Greece) is over 26 miles. Tradition says the original runner died delivering his message. Today the marathon race has become the blue ribbon climax of the summer Olympic Games, and the last lap is run before a cheering crowd inside the stadium.

We who are up in years and are looking soon to worship His Majesty before His throne are presently finishing our own marathons. In the next chapter you will learn about "John the Revelator" and will read his marvelous description of the heaven that awaits us. Now I would like to share with you how I think the apostle Paul himself might have envisioned a Christian's homegoing.

Paul, as we know from 1 Corinthians 9:24-26, was probably a fan of the ancient Olympic Games. I can imagine him writing in his old age to the Athenian Christians, "When you reach the end of your days and are finishing life's marathon race, you will be circling around the inside of an athletic stadium filled with people. Coming through the gate, you will have discovered that the King of kings is present in all His glory, together with a great cloud of witnesses from every tribe and nation in the world. They will now be clapping joyously for you—yes, you—as you pace around the track. They will be shouting to you, 'Congratulations, faithful one! A fine race! Well run! Good show! Glory, Hallelujah!' And then as you break the finish tape they will be waving and calling to you, 'Welcome in the Name of Jesus. Now join us, and enter into the Joy of your Lord!' "

Meanwhile, to come back to the present on mother earth, many of us who are children of God have found that *growing old is the best part of life.* Do you consider that a rash statement? Examine it. Make full allowance for the underside: the gradual weakening of the bodily systems, the danger of illness, the shortness of breath, the fading of memory. Our eyes, ears, and limbs—especially our fingers—don't work as well as they did. Our hair is whitening, our skin is wrinkling, our steps are slower. We pick up the phone and call someone, then forget what we wanted to say. We walk into a store and can't remember what we were looking for. If we wish to complain, there is plenty of subject matter.

But don't pity us too much. I have an elderly friend with a bad heart condition, yet when he smiles and shakes my hand, his grip is firm and strong. My old friend is getting medical help. We're all getting medical help, and we're grateful. But when I say we're having our best years, that's only part of the picture.

We have peace. We have joy. We have rest. We have family love. We have stopped chasing after flying goals. Hopefully, we are out of the child-rearing business. We have enough to live on—barely enough, perhaps, but not to worry. They are not going to draft us. They are not going to foreclose on us.

We're not going to let them. You see, we are not called "Foxy Grandpa" and "Wily Grandma" for nothing! We have not lost our "smarts."

The advertisers fill our mailboxes and choke the Internet and coo into our telephones with all kinds of lures and bargains. It's all right, but they could save themselves millions of dollars by leaving us alone. We know what we want, and they don't. We're having fun—our way. Not Mr. Sinatra's way—more like our Lord's way.

I am assuming that you are a Christian; that is, you have chosen to make Jesus Christ the focal point of your life. In case you misunderstand, by "focal point" I mean Savior, Lord, Redeemer, Strong Tower, Victor, Deliverer, Benchmark, Apex, or any other expression that conveys the meaning that Jesus is Captain of your ship.

Being a Christian means you have cleared away the trash in your spiritual life. You have survived the threatening boulders and yawning pits that lay in your way. You have skirted around the quicksand of discouragement. You have waded through the sump of despair. You have scaled the Grand Tetons of competition. You have paddled through the treacherous River of Temptation without capsizing. You have swum the Hellespont of poverty and surmounted the disappointments of Poopout Hill. You have leaned on the Holy Spirit to get through the Wilderness of Sin. In stormy weather you grasped the strong hand of Jesus as the earth under your feet began to shake.

The forces of evil set traps for you. The prince of this world tried to demolish you. All hell seemed at times to be against you. The darkness tried to douse your light, puncture your reputation, disillusion your friends, but you held steady and kept going. When they pushed you to the ropes, you fought back. When they brought you to your knees in seeming failure, you reached out for the hand of God, and He raised you up.

Congratulations! Today you are a living witness to the survival power of God's Word and the matchless love of Jesus. As you lie on your bed in the middle of the night, unable to sleep, the Almighty Himself is smiling on you, offering you a word of encouragement, saying to you something like, "Brother, Sister, I'm not through with you. There are people who need you. Children need you. Teenagers need you. They may not be sure they need you, but they do. It doesn't matter that you're not the 'person in charge' any more. There is room for the advice you can give, and you know how to give it without irritating them. Children would like to kiss you if you will let them. Take joy! I am with you, and I am smiling on your witness."

Faithfulness! Just to see you walking into church and taking your seat is reassuring to younger people. ("He/she still believes all that after so many years?!") You build young people's confidence in the gospel that has obviously worked for good in your own life. They observe you praying and singing in God's house, and listening to the message preached by a person perhaps decades younger than you. You show them that Jesus Christ is the same yesterday, today, and forever.[1] When you are invited to speak, and you begin your response with "Praise the Lord," you are breaking new ground for the generation that hears you.

We older people are examples of faithfulness not only in church and not only to our God; we are also examples to our families, our neighbors, our old buddies from work, our contemporaries, and our communities. We are programmed not to quit. We are simply not ready for the boneyard yet. There are millions of young people in our cities who have never heard of the joy of faithfulness. We want to help them find it. We want to show them what Jesus showed us, that the filling of the Spirit of God is a blessing that lasts.

Politically, older adults have moved into a position of signal importance in North America as we begin the third millennium.* Their numbers are growing at three times the rate of the natural population. Over-65 folks have reached a number in the United States that surpasses the entire population of Canada—and 600,000 of them are millionaires!

So do these seniors all go to church? No. Seven out of ten do not.[2] Some churches have changed their programs, trying to adapt in ways that will attract the "dropouts." Some have even changed their theology to "fit the times." But let's face it: Nothing truly reaches the sinful human heart except the gospel, and nothing will truly wash away sin except the blood of Jesus Christ.

For the sake of that gospel many Christians are enduring persecution and hard times in today's world. Even in our own country the environment seems to have changed its attitude toward Christians. What we always considered unacceptable behavior is now a brazen habit with many. Christian values seem not to be favored by the citizenry. The social climate gives no undergirding support to moral behavior.

While we enjoy our Indian-summer years, we can do something about that: not by nostalgically yearning for "the good old days," but simply by pointing people to Jesus. Believe it or not, people will listen to you. Years later they will repeat what Grandpa or Grandma said and take comfort in it. Bread cast upon the water returns.

Practically speaking, we can be a Big Brother or Big Sister to kindergarten children. We can visit shut-ins and read to them. We can write encouraging letters to the editor. We can make friends with the other older folks under our roof. We can thank storekeepers for their discounts. Most important of all, we can keep smiles on our faces.

---

* To meet the challenges of our new century, many new Christian organizations of older people are being formed today with emphasis on evangelism, outreach, service, fellowship, and spiritual growth. For information about and a description of one of them, the Christian Association of Senior Adults (CASA), see the appendix on page 209.

We're pilgrims on the journey of the narrow road,
And those who've gone before us line the way,
Cheering on the faithful, encouraging the weary,
Their lives a stirring testament to God's sustaining grace.

Surrounded by so great a cloud of witnesses,
Let us run the race not only for the prize;
But as those who've gone before us, let us leave to those
  behind us,
The heritage of faithfulness passed on through godly lives.

O may all who come behind us find us faithful;
May the fire of our devotion light their way.
May the footprints that we leave lead them to believe
And the lives we live inspire them to obey.

After all our hopes and dreams have come and gone,
And our children sift through all we've left behind,
May the clues that they discover, and the mem'ries they
  uncover
Become the light that leads them to the road we each
  must find.[3]
  —"Find Us Faithful," words and music by Jonathan
Mohr

Best of all, as we grow older we have our God—Father,
Son, and Holy Spirit—the God of the Scriptures and the God
who made us. Through all the years, those of plenty and those
not so plentiful, we have leaned on His goodness, and He has
not failed us. *God is faithful. He comes through. Gloria in
excelsis Deo.*

23

THE JOY OF HEAVEN

❧

Lord of the far horizons,
Give us the eyes to see
Over the verge of the sundown
The beauty that is to be.

—BLISS CARMAN (1861–1929)

The late J.B. Phillips was one of the last century's better translators of the New Testament. He has given us a stirring rendition of the apostle John's resplendent description of heaven that is found in the last two chapters of the book of Revelation. For a prophetic way to start this chapter, here it is:

> I heard a great voice from the throne crying, "See!
> The home of God is with men, and he will live
> among them. They shall be his people, and God
> himself shall be with them, and will wipe away
> every tear from their eyes. Death shall be no more,
> and never again shall there be sorrow or crying or
> pain. For all those former things are past and
> gone…See! I am making all things new!…"
>   Then he [an angel] carried me away in spirit to
> the top of a vast mountain, and pointed out to me the
> city, the holy Jerusalem, descending from God out
> of Heaven, radiant with the glory of God. Her bril-

liance sparkled like a very precious jewel with the
clear light of crystal....

The one who was talking to me had a golden rod in
his hand with which to measure the city, its gateways
and its wall....The wall itself was built of translucent
stone, while the city was of purest gold, with the
brilliance of glass. The foundation stones of the wall
of the city were fashioned out of every kind of precious stone. The first foundation-stone was jasper,
the second sapphire, the third chalcedony, the fourth
emerald, the fifth onyx, the sixth carnelian, the sev-
enth goldstone, the eighth beryl, the ninth topaz, the
tenth green goldstone, the eleventh turquoise, and
the twelfth amethyst. The twelve gates were twelve
pearls, each gate made of a single pearl....

I could see no Sanctuary in the city, for the Lord,
the Almighty God, and the Lamb are themselves its
Sanctuary. The city has no need for the light of sun
or moon, for the splendour of God fills it with light
and its radiance is the Lamb....

Nothing that has cursed mankind shall exist any
longer; the throne of God and of the Lamb shall be
within the city. His servants shall worship him; they
shall see his face, and his Name will be upon their
foreheads. Night shall be no more,...for the Lord
God will shed his light upon them and they shall
reign as kings for timeless ages."[1]

One exciting day soon, those now living whose names are
in the Lamb's book of life and who have been redeemed by
His blood will witness that glorious sight. Our faith tells us
that we earthbound sinners who have repented and trusted
Christ for our salvation will be not just admitted, but welcomed into that incredible city with music and shouts of joy.
Our cares will all be gone. Why? Because by the grace of our

God who smiles we have become children of the Light, set free and born from above to eternal life!

If that isn't cause for thanksgiving and laughter, I don't know what is. We probably will all have the same thought: "What am I doing here?!"

All those unfulfilled prospects of earth will come to us fulfilled in heaven. Birth defects and limb losses we carried through life will have disappeared forever. Did we strive for medals and awards and fail to qualify for them? The medals and awards of heaven will be better. Poetry we couldn't seem to write will flow from us. Knotty problems we never did solve will suddenly unravel. Differences with fellow Christians will be gone. Skills we struggled to master will be ours to use. Goals we set ourselves to achieve, mountains we sought to climb, will all be topics of laughter. The ravages of disease, migraine headaches, low IQ's, depression, and even hangnails will have been corrected and will have vanished forever.

Just for fun I dug out my collection of hymnbooks to see how the hymn- and songwriters have described heaven over the years. I had no idea there were so many hymns concerning heaven. Almost all the songs were about seeing Jesus there. They wanted to be near Him, to touch Him, to listen to Him. Some songs dwelt on the awesomeness of the heavenly Father. Many of the writers sang about a river flowing through heaven. Some placed emphasis on heaven as a place of rest. Others wrote about the music of heaven. And all of them spoke of it as a place of great joy. Things to do, places to go, wonders to examine, challenges to take up!

But now let us pause a moment. We need to listen to an old Negro spiritual that contains these words: "Heaven! Heaven! Ever'body talkin' 'bout Heaven ain't goin' there! Heaven..." That truth will one day confront all six billion people now living out their days on the earth's surface. There are people for whom the Bible is trash, but they may still maintain that heaven will become theirs by right. They will have "earned it" and will "deserve it" because of what they have "had to put up with" on earth, if for no other reason. What's more, they don't intend to let anyone try to deprive them of heaven. When the saints go marching in, they will be "right there, you bet." Or so they think.

That is probably as big a mistake as it is to believe there is no such place as heaven. We all know that what happens to us after death is in God's hands, not ours. He made us. He gave us life and turned us loose, allowing us free choice to accept or reject His gift of salvation through His Son. How are we doing? What have we learned, and what are we believing?

Roland Bainton tells us that when Thomas Hooker, the liberty-loving English preacher (who brought his flock to the New World and became one of the founders of Connecticut) lay dying in his home in Hartford in 1647, his friends gathered around his bedside and sought to comfort him.

"Brother Hooker," they said, "you are now going to receive your reward."

The rugged old Puritan founder took his time, but he finally sat up, looked sternly at them, and said, "I go to receive mercy."[2]

What a thrill to find a human being who isn't trying to push a track record, but is willing to cut the boasting, bow the head, and throw himself or herself utterly and totally on the grace and mercy of the unseen God. Many people think of heaven as a place of merit they can achieve for themselves by running up brownie points and carrying out good and generous deeds while on earth. Surely God would reward them for their kindness to others, wouldn't He? What kind of God is He?

They are in for two surprises. One has to do with God's plan of salvation but has nothing to do with our "good works" or "benevolent nature." God operates over a different wavelength. He peoples heaven with folks who believe His Son, love His Son, trust His Son, and have faith in His Son. These things are a long way from being a "nice guy," sharing a pizza with a sibling, or endowing an institution and naming it after oneself. God is not a copilot, and He has no copilots. He is the supreme Lord of all, or as the early Hawaiian converts used to refer to Him, the "Big Kahuna." He is worthy, almighty, beloved. We glorify Him because of who He is, and because we would rather glorify Him than ourselves.

The other surprise has to do with the bald truth that hell is real and substantial. It is not the figment of a warped and twisted imagination. Now this is a book about the God who smiles, not about the temperature of hell. I would however point out one fact that is relevant to the joys of heaven. It is that *the existence of hell proves we have freedom to choose* where we spend eternity. If there were no hell, there would be no such freedom.

Another important fact is that *the choices of time are binding in eternity*. My years as a newspaperman taught me something about crime, and postgraduate studies taught me something about cause and effect.

Deeds leave their mark. A human being who kills another does something that cannot be undone, ever. Let the warning stand. In a universe governed by a righteous God, "the judgments of the LORD are true and righteous altogether."[3]

That is how God has made His creation. Just as heaven is no myth, so hell is no joke. And while God did not originally make hell for us (but for the devil and his angels), God did make heaven and all its joys for us who love Him and are called according to His Name.

In his bestselling book *Angels: God's Secret Agents*, Billy Graham pointed out that angels carry messages.[4] If you look carefully at the word "evangelist," you will find the root word "angel" implanted in it. Angel comes from a common Greek word meaning "messenger" or "one sent." In ancient Greek literature an angel was always a messenger, whether human or supernatural.

That gives us a clue to the way we shall serve the Lord when we arrive in the heavenly precincts. Many people maintain they would be bored to death by the monotony of it all, but from my reading of the Bible I am convinced our life in heaven will be a time of supreme joy. And there's something else. Jesus, you recall, said that in the courts of heaven we would be like the angels, and since angels are messengers by definition, we can reasonably expect to be sent on missions wherever God in His wisdom chooses to send us. "His servants shall serve Him. They shall see his face."[5] Does that sound boring?

I talked with Gordon Cooper, one of the original seven American astronauts, after he had made his second orbital flight around the earth in a spacecraft. Colonel Cooper is a Christian. As he described his voyage in the Gemini 5 spacecraft some 150 miles above the earth, it did not sound boring to me.[6] And if you think heaven will be boring, you may have mixed it up with a different place.

There remains the question of death itself, and the Bible answers it beautifully. Death is not a "nothing"—it is the "last enemy," but it was defeated by Jesus Christ, *Christus Victor,* at His resurrection. It remains for us a portal to heaven, but for the Christian it is no longer a dread or a haunting threat. It brings sadness to those of us left behind when it takes our loved ones, but Jesus assured us that our mourning would be followed by the comforting presence of the Holy Spirit; and it is He who brings the joyful sunshine that comes "in the morning."

Back in the early 1950s, when I was a young pastor in my south Berkeley church, one of our most precious members died. This dear old grandmother, Grace Hubbard, spent her last years "tunking" up and down the front stairs of wooden houses, inviting everyone in our neighborhood to come to our services. She had a very gracious and genial nature. How we loved her, and how she loved Jesus!

In spite of my own sense of loss, I conducted Grace's funeral in a state of spiritual elation. I couldn't help it. I knew that death meant absolutely nothing to Grace Hubbard, that she was "winging it" in celestial spheres and having the time of her life. As best I could, I turned that funeral into a celebration of triumphant joy.

In John Bunyan's *Pilgrim's Progress*, when Christian and Hopeful finally enter the gates of the Heavenly City, they are greeted with harps and crowns, and "all the bells in the city rang for joy." When Mr. Valiant-for-truth passes over the river of death "all the trumpets sounded for him on the other side."[7]

We who are still here know that our summons will eventually come according to the laws of nature—unless in the meantime the Lord appears wreathed in clouds of glory. We Christians need not be afraid. Instead of dreading Shakespeare's "dusty death" or Longfellow's grim "reaper and sickle," we are answering a call to everlasting joy and glory in the presence of the One who made us. And praise God, we'll be joining all the saints, non-canonical, canonical, and super-canonical, who went before us.

The psalmist had it right: "In Your presence is fullness of joy; at Your right hand are pleasures forevermore."[8]

What a blast. Hallelujah!

Epilogue

Pour la Force sur Votre Voyage*

For by grace you have been saved through faith, and that not of yourselves; it is the gift of God, not of works, lest anyone should boast. For we are His workmanship, created in Christ Jesus for good works, which God prepared beforehand that we should walk in them.
—Ephesians 2:8-10

The love of God has been poured out in our hearts by the Holy Spirit who was given to us.
—Romans 5:5

I have been crucified with Christ; it is no longer I who live, but Christ lives in me; and the life which I now live in the flesh I live by faith in the Son of God, who loved me and gave Himself for me.
—Galatians 2:20

"Come to Me, all you who labor and are heavy laden, and I will give you rest. Take My yoke upon you and learn from Me, for I am gentle and lowly in heart, and you will find rest for your souls. For My yoke is easy and My burden is light."
—Matthew 11:28-30

All this from the God who smiles!

---

*For strength on your journey.

Afterthoughts:

The Human Smile

❧

A merry heart makes a cheerful countenance.

—Proverbs 15:13

STUDY SHOWS SMILES ON DOWNWARD TREND

NEW YORK: Citing a new statistical study, the North American Academy today announced a dramatic decrease in the amount of smiling being done by Americans and Canadians.

Using sample surveys from key states and provinces, the latest summary estimates that one-sixth of the North American population has given up smiling altogether. This contrasts with the one-tenth figure released by the same statistical team in 1980.

According to Dr. Herman Gedankenspritzer, the study's head statistical consultant, the serious drop in numbers of smiling people can possibly be attributed to dietary changes caused by recent fluctuations in the organic food supply. These fluctuations are in turn thought to be related to weather disturbances in Central America from the La Niña phenomenon.

In the year 1980, sample figures from NAA Smile Centers in Collinsville, Connecticut; Enid, Oklahoma; Burlington, Ontario; and Milpitas, California were extrapolated to give an estimated total of 1,948,121,002 positive (as opposed to negative) smiles per day on the faces of the North American populace.

The new survey, conducted in the same communities during the year 2000 and using the latest available technology, shows that the number of smiles per day has dropped to a shocking 1,302,477,001, reports Gedankenspritzer. This downward trend is projected to continue indefinitely. "People just aren't smiling any more!" explains Gedankenspritzer.

Other investigations by different organizations have pointed to social causes for the unsmiling phenomenon, such as the Pokémon explosion, the income tax debate, poorly-buttered popcorn, dull preaching in churches, and the total lack of humor in network television newscasts. One unexplored factor was mentioned by dental statistician Samuel Eventeeth, D.D.S. He reported that most dental patients told pollsters that, even after undergoing expensive dental work, they had stopped smiling because "there was nothing whatever to smile about."

This conclusion seems to contradict an actual postelection Gallup Poll from this year that indicates the American people are not really depressed at all. In fact, when questioned, 90 percent of those Americans surveyed "supported" or "strongly supported" the principles of honesty, democracy, moral courage, patriotism, caring for friends and family, and acceptance of all people regardless of race and ethnicity.

History Professor F. Phwat of Bunkum Center Junior College, Bunkum Center, Arkansas, recently entered the discussion by claiming that smile loss in North America originated with early European emigrants. Phwat attributes the fame of Leonardo da Vinci's *Mona Lisa* to the fact that she is smiling, "and smiles were a virtually unknown phenomenon in sixteenth-century Europe." In support of this he claims that no other smiling European pictures were painted in the sixteenth century "or have been since." This claim has been vigorously denied by art historians and consultants in Prague, Milan, Paris, and St. Petersburg..."

Well, all that was a spoof of course, and you will forgive me, but it does highlight what could happen if our facial muscles were suddenly to cease functioning in ways that bring on smiles and laughter. Something irreplaceable would go out of our human existence. A recent article in *Men's Health* magazine (no spoof) reports that Dr. Stanley Tam of Loma Linda University, California, tested 48 heart-attack survivors for a year, placing half of them in a room watching a comedy video of their choice for 30 minutes a day. The other half were not allowed to watch anything funny. (Someone suggested they were watching CBS.) After 12 months, only two patients in the first group had suffered another heart attack, compared to ten in the second group. Dr. Tam concluded, "Daily laughter seems to help restore brain neurotransmitters that help in coping with stress."[1]

I would say it does more than that. Smiles and laughter make life endurable for millions of people who otherwise would spend their days climbing walls, biting nails, and annoying other people. As the Irishman said, "If laughin' ain't the gift o' the livin' God, I don't know wot is!"

SMILES MAKE A DIFFERENCE

More than once a smile has averted manslaughter. The most famous fictional instance is described in Owen Wister's pioneer Western novel *The Virginian,* published in 1902. The central figure in Wister's story was playing cards in a back room, and it was his turn to bet. Instead he paused, whereupon another player named Trampas rebuked him with an uncomplimentary description of his ancestry. The Virginian reached for his pistol but did not point it. Instead he looked across the table at Trampas and said, *"When you call me that, smile."* [2] (From such scenes has emerged the American language.)

Martial, an ancient Roman (not a Christian) wrote, "A face that cannot smile is never good."[3]

Joseph Addison, eighteenth-century English essayist and poet, wrote, "What sunshine is to flowers, smiles are to humanity. They are but trifles, to be sure, but the good they do is inconceivable."[4]

I find it fascinating how a smile can change destiny. In 1940 I was working in Columbia, Missouri and had the privilege of hearing Dale Carnegie lecture at the University of Missouri. I shall always remember one sentence of that lecture. He said, "Everything I teach in my books and in my lectures I learned from Jesus." I have asked permission to reprint a passage from Carnegie's 1936 bestselling book, *How to Win Friends and Influence People,* in which he quotes from a letter written to him by an American businessman, William B. Steinhardt.

> "I seldom smiled at my wife or spoke two dozen words to her before leaving for business. After hearing you speak, I thought I would try it for a week. As I sat down to breakfast, I greeted my wife with a 'Good morning, my dear,' and smiled at her. She was bewildered. She was shocked. I told her in future she could expect this as a regular occurrence. I smiled at the Curb Exchange at men who never saw me smile. I found everybody was smiling back at me. I now treat those who come with grievances in a cheerful manner and smile as I listen to them. I find that smiles are bringing me dollars, many dollars, every day. I am a totally different man, richer in friendships and happiness."[5]

Too simple, you say? Too contrived? Try it yourself. Frank Fletcher, another twentieth-century businessman, wrote after listening to Carnegie, "A smile costs nothing, but creates much. It enriches those who receive, without impoverishing those who give. It happens in a flash, and the memory of it sometimes lasts forever. It cannot be bought, begged, borrowed, or stolen, for it is something that is no earthly good to anybody till it is given away!"[6]

GIVING SMILES AWAY

When God finally allowed me to break into print after 25 futile years of rejections, He didn't stop at that. He said, "Now that you know how it is done, I want you to spend time helping other writers of Mine to be published." Thousands of good Christians today want to be able to write about what God has done for them but feel as helpless as I did about breaking into print. "Help them," God seemed to say. "Show them how to do it."

Well, I did and still do, having taught hundreds of writing groups from Nome, Alaska, to Auckland, New Zealand, to Durban, South Africa. These groups have learned how to form guilds and to help each other with their writing, and how to understand and penetrate the publishing market, Christian and secular. The best advice I give them is, "Getting into print is like getting into heaven. It's not what you do, it's who you know!"

What has smiling to do with it? It is at the very heart of the learning process. Today Christian writers' guilds are expanding in many parts of the world, and the key to the guild is invariably the individual critique unit, where very small groups get together and the people read and help each other with their writing. Here smiles of encouragement are absolutely vital. Corrections and suggestions are couched in positive expressions. Ways of improvement, additional copy, elimination of weak spots, and suggestions for possible markets always need to be accompanied by smiles.

People are very sensitive about their writings because what they write is what they are. A smile of encouragement from anyone will keep me reworking my own material until it seems to sing. (Always it should be remembered that the basic purpose of a Christian writers' guild is not just to see writing skills improved or copy marketed and published, but to build up Christians in the most holy faith and give them confidence in God not only about their ability to write, but about their ability to help others through their writing.)

DOES THE SMILE CREATE DESTINY?

It's a nice question: In the remarkable happenings of life, does the smile create destiny or does destiny create the smile? Samuel Zwemer said something like this: "You can offer a Bible to a Muslim, and he'll take it—if you smile." If Regis Philbin were to say to a television game contestant, "You have just won a million dollars!" without some kind of a smile on his face, my guess is that he would hear about it sharply. His smile may have won him his position in the first place.

The deeper question as to whether smiles and laughter actually fill important functions in the affairs of life is something that has challenged human thought for centuries. Overlooking the bray of a donkey, animals do not smile (Darwinians note), but have other ways of expressing pleasure. Somewhere I read Samuel Butler's acid remark that "all animals except man know that the principal business of life is to enjoy it." A bad call. The trouble is that in a blighted world such as ours, animals find much of their enjoyment in digesting each other.

CHRISTIANS HAVE THE BEST REASONS TO SMILE

To sum up, the human smile is one of the most wonderful things in all of God's creation, and *we Christians have more to smile about than anybody else.* One of the greatest challenges facing civilized society today is to turn the church inside out and lift the roof off its top so the sunshine can get in. William

Barclay says, "The Christian is the laughing cavalier of Christ." God grant it may be so.

Thinking of attending a Bible study class? Do it with a smile.

Thinking of learning to teach the Bible to small groups? Do it with a smile.

Wondering about supporting a missionary overseas, or becoming one yourself? Do it with a smile.

Considering taking an interest in children's recreational activities, or visiting senior retirement groups, or traveling on a Bible tour to the Holy Land? Do it with a smile.

Want to invite friends at work to your home for a specialized Bible study? Do it with a smile.

Want to learn more about what Chuck Colson calls "developing a Christian worldview?" Do it with a smile.

Thinking of taking adult classes at a Christian school or college, or becoming involved in your local church choir, or assisting your pastor by cataloging his library, or helping to build an addition to your church, or learning foreign languages in preparation for overseas service, or joining a historical or literary group, or learning to play musical instruments for worship, or joining an evangelistic team, or serving on a church board? Do it with a smile.

Or perhaps you are not thinking of the church at all, but want to become a homemaker, wife, and mother, or go into a professional field, or start your own business, or enter the high-tech industry, or take up scientific study, or elementary teaching, or engineering, or accounting, or software, or the military profession, or the teaching of mathematics, or medical practice, or enter government service, or any other line of work. Do you love the Lord? Then do it with a smile. That takes 17 muscles; a frown takes 43, according to Gyles Brandreth *(Your Vital Statistics)*. And may the Joy of the Lord go with you.

Appendix
Information About CASA

Let me tell you about one of the new Christian organizations of older people that has been formed. It is named CASA, the Christian Association of Senior Adults, and it has already spread to 32 states, Canada, and Australia (I am a part of this organization as a member of the board of reference). Thousands of seniors are flocking to their popular meetings.

The whole purpose of this association is the honoring of God and God's faithful servants, and emphasizing the importance of our continued faithfulness toward God in our senior years.* The address of CASA is 27601 Forbes Road, #49, Laguna Niguel, California, 92677. The telephone is 888-200-8552.

Among the projects now active in CASA are leadership training, ministry resources for evangelical pastors and leaders of senior ministries, and program development for new associations. To me it is beautiful to see people of great talent putting those rusty talents to work in providing rich spiritual opportunities for eager brothers and sisters of advanced age. The seniors in turn are being encouraged to pray for and develop Christian leadership among the younger people in their own churches.

Two general groups are now functioning as "middle adults" (ages 59 to 69) and "mature adults" (ages 70+). They have been producing videotapes, books, and a publication, the *Senior Energizers.*

CASA began when three California churches met in 1982 to discuss the possibility of a Jamboree for southern California's older church population. This has now led to annual "Life Celebrations" that bring over 2,000 seniors together from all over the southwestern United States, and they are now moving eastward. These gatherings are enormously inspiring occasions, as they provide, among other things, opportunities to fellowship with other seniors and to sing the familiar anthems, hymns, and gospel songs of our younger days. We have fun!

---

* One of CASA's theme songs, "Find Us Faithful," is on page 190 of this book. This song expresses the purpose of the organization better than any words on a page.

Notes

CHAPTER 1: DOES HE OR DOESN'T HE?

1. James Moffatt, *A New Translation of the Bible* (London: Hodder & Stoughton, 1950).

CHAPTER 2: WHAT IS THE GREAT JOY?

1. Alexander Schmemann, in "For the Life of the World, Sacraments and Orthodoxy," 1973. Reprinted in *Alive Now* magazine, Nov.-Dec., 1999. Used by permission of St. Vladimir's Seminary Press, Crestwood, NY.
2. Job 38:4,5.
3. See Job 38:7.
4. From "A Conversation with Cynthia Wilson-Felder," in *Alive Now* magazine, Nov.-Dec., 1999, pp. 18-23.
5. See Will Durant, *The Story of Philosophy*, pp. 301-334.
6. Ezekiel 18:24.
7. Hebrews 10:31.

CHAPTER 3: THE GLORIOUS CREATION

1. *The Brothers Karamazov.*
2. See Revelation 4:11 KJV.
3. See A.J. Toynbee, *A Study of History* (abridged) (London: Oxford University Press, 1947), p. 61; Sir James Jeans, *The Mysterious Universe* (New York: Macmillan, 1933), pp. 1-2.
4. Jeans, *The Mysterious Universe.*
5. James Drever Sr., *The Psychology of Everyday Life* (London: Methuen, 1948), p.8.

CHAPTER 4: GOD SMILES ON HIS WORD

1. Luke 3:21,22.
2. See Acts 17:18.
3. Revelation 22:3.
4. Matthew 11:28-30.

CHAPTER 5: GOD SMILES ON HIS WARRIORS

1. 2 Corinthians 10:4 KJV.
2. Cecil Woodham-Smith, *Florence Nightingale* (London: Constable, 1950).
3. J.H. Oldham, *Real Life Is Meeting* (London: The Sheldon Press, 1942), p. 21.
4. See Ephesians 6:10-18.
5. John 16:33.
6. 1 Peter 1:8 KJV.
7. Dora Greenwell, *Essays* (New York: Alexander Strahan, 1866).
8. Psalm 23:5 KJV.
9. Judges 5:20 NIV.
10. Nehemiah 4:17-29; 8:10.
11. See 1 Samuel 16:13.
12. Gustaf Aulen, *Christus Victor* (London: SPCK, 1940).

CHAPTER 6: GOD SMILES THROUGH HIS SON

1. John 16:22 RSV.
2. Mark 1:15 NIV.
3. Charles Colson and Nancy Pearcey, *How Now Shall We Live?* (Wheaton, IL: Tyndale, 1999).
4. Jeremiah 29:13.
5. John 15:5.
6. Andrew Murray, *The True Vine* (Chicago: Moody Press, 1982).
7. Norman P. Grubb, *Rees Howells, Intercessor* (London: Lutterworth Press, 1953).

CHAPTER 7: GOD SMILES ON HIS HOUSE

1. 2 Chronicles 6:18.
2. Matthew 26:61.
3. 1 Corinthians 6:19.
4. Matthew 18:20.
5. 1 Peter 2:5.

6. Henry Suso, "Rapture," in Georges A. Barrois, ed., *Pathways of the Inner Life* (Indianapolis: Bobbs-Merrill), pp. 95-96.

7. Reproduced in *Spiritual Disciplines*, Sherwood E. Wirt, ed., vol. 1 of *Christian Heritage Classics,* (Westchester, IL: Crossway Books, 1983), pp. 24-25, emphasis added.

8. Dorothy Sayers, tr., *Dante Alighieri. The Comedy*, Cantica 3, Canto 27 (New York: Penguin, 1976), emphasis added.

9. Psalm 16:11.

CHAPTER 8: GOD SMILES IN THE STARS

1. Amos 3:3.

2. 2 Thessalonians 2:7 KJV.

3. Isaiah 55:8 KJV.

4. John 16:23.

5. See Psalm 2:1.

6. Psalm 2:4.

7. J.I. Packer, *Knowing God* (Downers Grove, IL: InterVarsity Press, 1973).

CHAPTER 9: GOD SMILES ON RADIANT LOVE

1. Miguel de Cervantes, *The Adventures of Don Quixote de la Mancha* (written 1605–15).

2. Ephesians 5:25.

3. Ed and Gaye Wheat, *Intended for Pleasure* (Old Tappan, NJ: Fleming H. Revell, 1981), p. 144.

4. George Bernard Shaw, *Pygmalion*, Act 5 (First produced in 1912).

5. Tim and Beverly LaHaye, *The Act of Marriage* (Grand Rapids, MI: Zondervan, 1976); Clifford and Joyce Penner, *The Gift of Sex* (Waco, TX: Word, 1981); Ed and Gaye Wheat, *Intended for Pleasure.*

CHAPTER 10: GOD SMILES ON CHILDREN

1. Proverbs 22:6.

2. Jeremiah 6:16.

3. Luke 1:46,47.

4. Luke 2:10,11.
5. See Luke 2:41-52.
6. See Titus 3:5.

CHAPTER 11: GOD SMILES WHEN WE COME TO HIM

1. Romans 9:16 KJV.
2. Luke 15:10.
3. From C.S. Lewis, *God in the Dock* (Grand Rapids, MI: Eerdmans, 1970), p. 261 forward.
4. From *Decision* magazine, December, 1968, p. 7, emphasis added. By permission.
5. Published by Macmillan: New York, 1945, emphasis added. By permission.
6. From Helga B. Henry, *Mission on Main Street* (Chicago: W.A. Wilde, 1955), p. 72, emphasis added. By permission of the author.
7. From Aaron N. Meckel, *New Day in Evangelism* (New York: E.P. Dutton, 1947) emphasis added. By permission.
8. From *Decision* magazine, July, 1962, p. 8, emphasis added. By permission.
9. From Curtis Mitchell, *Those Who Came Forward* (Philadelphia: Chilton Books, 1966), p. 153, emphasis added. By permission.

CHAPTER 12: WHEN SMILING LEADS TO LAUGHTER

1. William Temple, *Christianity and Social Order* (London: SCM Press, 1950), p. 52.
2. James S. Stewart, *Walking with God* (Edinburgh: St. George's Press, 1993), pp. 153-154.
3. Norman P. Grubb, *Rees Howells, Intercessor* (London: Lutterworth Press, 1953), p. 11.

CHAPTER 13: DOES GOD'S SMILE REALLY MATTER TO US?

1. Jonah 1:1-3.
2. Acts 9:15.
3. Jonah 4:3.
4. Acts 13:52.

5. Acts 14:17 NIV.
6. Acts 16:25.
7. Acts 16:34.
8. Acts 16:37-40.
9. See Acts 27:34.
10. Acts 28:15.
11. 2 Corinthians 4:8-10; 6:10; 7:4 NIV.

CHAPTER 14: THE JOY FACTOR

1. Acts 2:26,28 NIV.
2. Acts 2:47 NIV.
3. Romans 11:34.
4. John 20:20 NIV.
5. From "Riches of Glory," words by H.B. Hartzler, n.d.
6. Galatians 4:19.
7. This quotation is not validated.
8. 2 Corinthians 6:4,10.
9. Hebrews 12:2.
10. Ken Blue, *Healing Spiritual Abuse* (Downers Grove, IL: InterVarsity Press, 1993).
11. Psalm 43:4.
12. John 16:24.
13. Blue, *Healing Spiritual Abuse*.

CHAPTER 15: THE JOY OF OBEDIENCE

1. Jeremiah 42:6.
2. Luke 10:28.
3. Galatians 2:16.
4. Matthew 11:30.
5. See Hebrews 11:15,16.
6. Ed and Gaye Wheat, *Intended for Pleasure* (Old Tappan, N.J.: Fleming H. Revell), 1981.
7. Charles Hodge, *Systematic Theology* (Grand Rapids, MI: Baker Book House, 1988).
8. Mark 14:36.
9. Hebrews 12:2, italics added.

CHAPTER 16: THE JOY OF PRAYER

1. Norman P. Grubb, *Rees Howells, Intercessor* (London: Lutterworth Press, 1953), p. 43, emphasis added.
2. James 4:2,3,6; 5:16; emphasis added.
3. Lady Julian of Norwich, *Revelations of Divine Love* (London: Methuen, 1911).
4. Ole Hallesby, *Prayer* (Minneapolis: Augsburg, 1937), p. 37.
5. See Matthew 28:9.
6. Charles G. Finney, *Memoirs* (New York: A.S. Barnes, 1970), p. 10.
7. Hallesby, *Prayer.*
8. Revelation 5:8,9, emphasis added.

CHAPTER 17: THE JOY OF FRIENDSHIP

1. John 15:13-16; 16:27.
2. Matthew 5:25.
3. See *The Arabian Nights or Thousand and One Nights,* tr. from the French of Antoine Galland, 1705.
4. Ecclesiasticus 44:1,2.
5. Ecclesiasticus 6:14-17, emphasis added.
6. Genesis 2:22,23.
7. Proverbs 18:24.
8. 1 Timothy 2:3,4.

CHAPTER 18: WHEN GOD STOPPED SMILING

1. Titus Lucretius Carus (approximately 95–55 B.C.), Epicurean poet who lived in Rome. Almost nothing is known of his life except Jerome's brief note. A letter of Cicero to his brother reveals that Lucretius' poem was being read in 54 B.C.
2. See the biographical note in vol. 12 of *Great Books of the Western World,* "Lucretius on the Nature of Things," tr. by H.A.J. Munro (Chicago: Encyclopedia Britannica Inc., 1982), p. ix.

CHAPTER 19: EPIPHANY AT WATERLOO STATION

1. See John 16:33 NIV; 16:33; 10:10.
2. Zechariah 4:6.
3. Romans 5:5.
4. Francis Schaeffer, *Complete Works,* vol. 3 (Westchester, IL: Crossway Books, 1982), p. 355.

CHAPTER 20: FACING THE REAL QUESTION

1. Matthew 10:16.
2. Blaise Pascal, *Pensees*, no. 894. In *Pensees and the Provincial Letters* (New York: Modern Library, 1941), p. 314.
3. Romans 5:5.
4. Psalm 43:4.

CHAPTER 21: WHEN LIFE TUMBLES IN

1. Psalm 31:2.
2. See Hebrews 12:11.
3. Isaiah 53:3-5 NIV.
4. 1 John 2:1.
5. James 1:2,3,12 NIV.

CHAPTER 22: THE JOY OF FAITHFULNESS

1. Hebrews 13:8.
2. *Energizing Seniors,* CASA newsletter.
3. Words and music by Jonathan Mohr. Copyright © 1987 Jonathan Mark Music and Birdwing Music. All rights reserved. Used by permission.

CHAPTER 23: THE JOY OF HEAVEN

1. Revelation 21:3-5,10,11,15,18-23; 22:3-5 PHILLIPS.
2. Roland Bainton, in lecture at Pacific School of Religion, Berkeley, CA, circa 1952.
3. Psalm 19:9.
4. Billy Graham, *Angels: God's Secret Agents* (Waco, TX: Word Publishing, 1994).
5. Revelation 22:3,4.
6. Gordon Cooper, "God and Man in Space," *Decision* magazine, March, 1966, p. 3.

7. John Bunyan, *The Pilgrim's Progress* (Chicago: John C. Winston, 1933).

8. Psalm 16:11.

AFTERTHOUGHTS: THE HUMAN SMILE

1. From *Energizing Seniors* magazine, Winter, 1999.

2. Owen Wister, *The Virginian, a Horseman of the Plains* (New York: Macmillan, 1970), p. 24.

3. Martial was a first-century A.D. Roman writer of epigrams. From *The New Dictionary of Thoughts* (Garden City, NY: Hanover House, 1960), p. 624.

4. Joseph Addison, in *FPA's Book of Quotations* (New York: Funk & Wagnalls, 1952), p. 733.

5. Dale Carnegie, *How to Win Friends and Influence People* (New York: Simon & Schuster, 1936), pp. 68-69.

6. Frank Fletcher, in Dale Carnegie, *How to win Friends...*

INDEX OF SCRIPTURE VERSES

OTHER HARVEST HOUSE READING

Jesus, Man of Joy
by Sherwood Wirt

To those of us who think of Jesus as humorless and unfeeling, Sherwood Wirt offers a fresh look at the most joyful man who ever lived. You will catch a vision of the passion, playfulness, and excitement of the Lord, and be reminded to enjoy the life He has given you to the fullest.

In the Footsteps of Jesus
by Bruce Marchiano

Bruce brings Jesus into clear focus, revealing the incredible joy, love, and sorrow He experienced. Bruce's conversational style and gripping storytelling give you a richer understanding of Jesus' humanity, deity, and message. *In the Footsteps of Jesus* is based on Bruce's portrayal of Jesus in *The Gospel According to Matthew* (The Visual Bible).

Jesus: Yesterday, Today, Forever
by Bruce Marchiano

Bruce's enthusiastic message of the joy and excitement of Jesus will touch your heart and soul and will encourage you to personally experience the man of miracles for yourself. Includes gripping photos from the *Matthew* and *Luke* films.

Grace Walk
by Steve McVey

What you've always wanted in the Christian life...but never expected. Let Christ and His joy live through you; let Him push aside your failures and self-sufficiency. Experience the grace walk, and know the spiritual fulfillment you have been striving for all along—but can never find outside of Jesus Christ.

The Father Heart of God
by Floyd McClung

The compassion of the Father enables us to overcome insecurity and the devastating effects of some of life's most painful experiences so we can experience the joyful life He has for us in Christ.